CONQUER PROCRASTINATION

CONQUER
PROCRASTINATION

Proven Strategies to Maintain Productivity
and Take Control of Your Life

Nadalie Bardo

ROCKRIDGE
PRESS

Interior and Cover Designer: Linda Snorina
Art Producer: Samantha Ulban
Editors: Carolyn Abate and Samantha Holland
Production Editor: Andrew Yackira

Copyright Page: Cover Illustration by © 2020 Hanna Barczyk
All other images used under license © Shutterstock
Author photo courtesy of Alana Thomson

ISBN: Print 978-1-64739-500-1 l eBook 978-1-64739-304-5
R0

To my mom—without you,

I wouldn't be here.

Thank you for teaching me

this one simple truth:

Whatever *is* meant for me,

will be mine.

CONTENTS

INTRODUCTION

THERE I WAS, sitting cross-legged with my laptop in the common room as the noise of my housemates washed over me. I don't know how I stayed up all night, or how I sat there staring at my laptop for 12 hours without getting anything done, but I did. I looked still and calm, but on the inside I was screaming my head off because I had a massive final paper due at noon the next day and I couldn't get started. Why did I wait until now? How did I let this happen again?

Somehow, with three hours to go, I hammered out the most perfect paper, and just barely got it turned in on time. Would you believe me if I told you that I got not one, but two As on this paper? I was an expert procrastinator; I'd bet against time and deadlines, used tactics to delay, and won again. But at what cost?

At first glance, that story has a happy ending. It may even lead you to conclude that procrastination isn't a problem. You might think to yourself after surviving similar situations, *It's okay—I still got it done.* But that's exactly how procrastination traps you, how it twists your view. You tell yourself that things worked out, so you keep doing it . . . until things don't work out. What my story doesn't share is how stressed I was during that time of my life, more stressed than I had ever been. I wasn't sleeping, I was partying to deal with it, and it was making me miserable. The following year, I made a choice that changed my life forever: I decided that I would no longer put things off until the last minute.

Thinking back, I probably didn't even recognize what I was doing as procrastination. All I knew was that I would no longer let this behavior drive me. I hope you're reading this book because you, too, have realized that procrastinating is not a sustainable way to get things done or accomplish your goals. It's not worth the stress, the drama, and the risk of losing everything because you were too rushed to do your best. So why do you keep playing the procrastination game?

The strategies in this book work—I'm living proof of that. As a former graduate student who's worked full-time and now runs an online business from home, I have made a lifelong commitment to conquering procrastination. On my blog, *It's All You Boo*, I help real people—students, parents, employees, entrepreneurs, and everyone in between—slay their goals with confidence and action. I'll share the same action-taking strategies with you to help you get things done, set goals, manage your time, get motivated, stay focused, and build momentum. Plus, with the guidance of leading psychologists, you'll finally understand why you procrastinate and how to break this habit for good.

Because you're reading this book, I know you are ready to kick procrastination out of your life. I'm so proud of you for making the choice to leave procrastination behind.

You can do this. You've already taken the first step!

CHAPTER 1

The Psychology of Procrastination

It happened *again*, didn't it?

You told yourself that you'd watch just one more episode, wait just one more day, do just one more errand. Then you'd be ready. And then you'd get started.

But you weren't ready, and maybe you still aren't. You didn't start; you put it off yet again. Or maybe you started, but now everything's so late that you're overwhelmed and discouraged. You're frustrated, feeling guilty, and feeling all sorts of shame. Why is it so hard to focus on what matters? Why does this keep happening?

Before we plunge into the answer, I want you to know one thing: The problem is not you. It's procrastination. You're familiar with the word, I'm sure. But it's important that you understand that procrastination is a habit. It's not who you are. You are not your habits. And you *can* lose this bad habit for good. Together, we'll begin by unpacking what procrastination is (and isn't). You'll discover the real reason you procrastinate and find out what kind of procrastination you're prone to. And those insights will empower you to stop procrastinating and start being productive. Ready to get started?

What Is Procrastination?

Let's do some word association. When I say "procrastination," what comes to mind? Let me guess. Do terms like "laziness," "lack of self-control," "disorganization," or "poor time-management skills" pop into your head? Perhaps you think procrastination springs from indifference, or that it's an innate personality flaw. You're not alone in thinking this way; that's what the collective consciousness believes about procrastination. Harsh, right? Thankfully, they're just shared myths. There's no reason to apply that derogatory language to you, or anyone else, when we procrastinate.

Psychologists offer us a more complex picture of procrastination, which we'll explore in this chapter. But first, let's simply define the term: Procrastination is a counterproductive putting off of, and an irrational delay to, action. It's a failure to start. It holds you back from accomplishing important tasks that you should, and could, get done.

WHAT PROCRASTINATION IS NOT

Procrastination expert and University of Calgary psychology researcher Piers Steel, PhD, explains that it isn't the delay or the action of putting off tasks that defines procrastination. Rather, the phenomenon is categorized by its irrational, self-sabotaging, and potentially harmful nature. In other words, not doing something right away, or at all, doesn't mean you're procrastinating. There are many positive reasons for waiting to perform a task, like managing priorities, working out scheduling conflicts, or taking time to prepare. You're only procrastinating if you've delayed a task that's in your best interest or your long-term benefit to complete, despite having the time and opportunity to do so. Let me repeat that: You had the time, you had the chance to accomplish it, but you didn't.

No, you were not too busy, nor were you too lazy. You procrastinated. But who hasn't? Will the non-procrastinator please stand up? Finding a true non-procrastinator is rare, and here's why: Professor Steel estimates that 95 percent of us procrastinate to some degree. His 2007 study, for example, concluded that between 80 to 95 percent of college students procrastinate (which is not shocking to anyone who's been to college). The truth is that procrastination is happening all around us. The great news for you is that even the most successful and accomplished people have to fight procrastination. The difference is that they win that fight. Just like you will after reading this book.

WHAT PROCRASTINATION LOOKS LIKE

We all experience our own challenges and situations, so it's not surprising that we all procrastinate differently, finding unique ways to delay completing things that we should—and could—get done. For example, maybe your house is the cleanest when you're avoiding doing something else, or maybe you're avoiding a task that is important, but that you don't enjoy. Some people just have trouble meeting deadlines, and no matter how much time they have, they always find themselves fighting against the clock to hand in assignments. Or perhaps you just keep checking social media—anything but starting that important task that's been on your to-do list for ages.

On the very extreme end, people who procrastinate will even put off critical medical appointments, delay trying to quit a harmful habit like smoking, avoid getting their car fixed, or wait on saving money for retirement. This is where procrastination behavior can become life-threatening. But even if we're not that far gone, the rest of us might risk our emotional and mental health, and potentially our relationships, when we procrastinate. So, why do we do it?

THE WORD, DEFINED

Merriam-Webster defines the verb procrastinate as "to put off intentionally the doing of something that should be done." Other definitions are "to defer action" and "delay." The word "procrastinate" was adopted by 16th-century English speakers from the Latin word *procrastinatus*, which is similarly defined. But let's take a closer look. "Pro-" as a prefix typically means support for something, with its origins in Latin meaning "forward." In this case, pro- applies to the Latin root *crastinus*, meaning "of tomorrow." When you put these two Latin words together, you get "for tomorrow." So, when you procrastinate, you are for tomorrow, not for today or now. Procrastination is also said to have roots in *akrasia*, the ancient Greek word that means "weakness of will" and "acting in a way contrary to one's sincerely held moral values." Sounds a lot like procrastination, doesn't it?

Why We Procrastinate

Spoiler alert: we all procrastinate for different reasons. In recent years, psychologists have been examining procrastination more and more as an emotional issue. This behavior is described as irrational—we said so a few paragraphs back, remember?—so of course emotions must be involved. Think about it: You instantly feel better when you procrastinate. But shortly after, you're hit with a stronger dose of shame, guilt, stress, anxiety, and other negative emotions. To cope, you procrastinate again, chasing the relief that comes from avoiding something you don't want to do. And the cycle continues. So, why start it at all? Let's take a look at the seven most common causes of procrastination.

BORING OR TEDIOUS TASKS

We often procrastinate tasks that we assume, or know from experience, to be boring or tedious. In this case, procrastination is the solution to doing something uncomfortable, unexciting, or not enjoyable. Sometimes our lack of genuine interest makes a task seem more tedious than it actually is. This reason for procrastinating is common for projects that require a lot of work over an extended period of time, like preparing to file your taxes or working on a household budget. These kinds of tasks require extended focus, dedication, and organization. Unless you're lucky enough to love bookkeeping—yes, some people do—completing these tasks can be a real challenge to your concentration.

AVOIDING NEGATIVE EMOTIONS

Okay, lean in a little closer; I'm going to tell you an important secret. When you procrastinate, *you're not avoiding doing a task*. Rather, you're actually avoiding the *feelings* that the task provokes in you: stress, fatigue, anxiety, frustration, discomfort, boredom, being overwhelmed, or even being challenged in an undesired way. For this reason, Carleton University psychologist and researcher Tim Pychyl, PhD, author of *Solving the Procrastination Puzzle: A Concise Guide to Strategies for Change*, describes procrastination as "an emotion-focused coping strategy." It's a way to feel good, instead of the perceived "bad" in the moment. Negative emotions can be unsettling. So, we use procrastination as a way to deal, even if it's just temporary relief.

FEELING OVERWHELMED

A major reason for not getting started is not knowing how, or where, to begin. This is especially true when a task feels too big, too important, or even too out of reach. Instead of putting in the work to establish a starting point or just diving in, we procrastinate to take a break from feelings of stress, pressure, and anxiety that the task evokes. Like all negative feelings that cause us to procrastinate, feeling overwhelmed can be a reasonable reaction. Or it could be mostly self-generated, obsessive overthinking, and indecision over a task that's not as big a deal as you make it out to be.

POOR DECISION-MAKING

Instead of using every opportunity to get started on a project, poor decision-makers choose to continue waiting, planning, or thinking. This tendency worsens if we lack a sense of urgency or feel that there's no real deadline or incentive to complete the task. It's even more common to underestimate how long tasks may take or how difficult they will be. The less time we give ourselves to complete an important task, the greater the pressure to complete it. And that higher pressure makes opting for procrastination even more tempting.

SELF-DOUBT AND LOW SELF-ESTEEM

It's easy to imagine how doing something new or challenging can cause us to doubt ourselves and our abilities. Thoughts and feelings of insecurity and anxiety can spiral and multiply when we are faced with an intimidating task. You might face limiting beliefs that range from, *I can't do this* to *I'm not good enough*. Sadly, putting things off only feeds the fire of your insecurities because you've accepted those limitations without trying to prove them wrong. If you already had low self-esteem or hold a negative perception of yourself to begin with, this pressure to procrastinate can be even worse. In that case, you might not be able to give yourself credit for past successes, or even see yourself as capable in the present.

FEAR OF FAILURE . . . OR SUCCESS

This is a big one. A fear of failure can be so much more intense than just worrying about making a mistake. It can be debilitating, especially because we often fear the emotions associated with failure as much as failure itself. Procrastination might be used to dodge feelings of disappointment, shame, defeat, anger, frustration, and other emotional outcomes associated with failing. If you fail publicly, the additional emotional strain may increase your worry of what others may think of you. You can even fear success because of your own beliefs that you're unworthy or undeserving. Instead of risking feeling these fears you might self-sabotage by procrastinating.

DISCONNECTED FROM OUR FUTURE SELVES

When we procrastinate, we put things off for temporary relief, despite creating future consequences for ourselves. So, why do we do it? A study by UCLA psychologist Hal Hershfield, PhD, offers an interesting explanation: We experience our present and future selves as separate beings. Being present-minded, we put off things that are in the distant future, like saving for retirement. That future me, the one who's retiring a few decades from now—that's somebody else, not me. It sounds kind of nutty, but MRI scans from this study prove it. When you think about your future self, your brain responds in a way that's similar to how it responds when you think about another person. If we don't form connections with our future selves, it's easy to make choices that don't consider who we'll be tomorrow.

WHY DO YOU PROCRASTINATE?

Because quiz-based learning is the best kind of learning, try this quiz to discover which causes of procrastination you most relate to. Score each statement from 1 to 5, with 1 being never, 2 rarely, 3 sometimes, 4 often, and 5 always.

1. **When I feel bored, I am easily distracted.**

   1   2   3   4   5

2. **I tell myself that I'll get started when I feel like it.**

   1   2   3   4   5

3. **If something is challenging, I put it off as long as I can.**

   1   2   3   4   5

4. **When facing a new task, I feel as if I don't know where to start.**

   1   2   3   4   5

5. **I'm scared I'll make the wrong choices.**

   1   2   3   4   5

6. **I misjudge how long completing a task will take.**

   1   2   3   4   5

7. **I'm afraid to fail or make mistakes.**

   1   2   3   4   5

8. **I worry that I'm a fraud and can't do this.**

   1   2   3   4   5

9. **I'd rather enjoy today and stress out tomorrow.**

   1   2   3   4   5

10. **I enjoy planning but can't seem to take action.**

    1   2   3   4   5

Which statements scored the highest?

1 AND 2: You might be procrastinating because you are avoiding feeling negative emotions like boredom, stress, and anxiety.

3 AND 4: The source of your procrastination is likely due to feelings of being overwhelmed and pressured.

5 AND 6: You might be putting things off because you're making poor decisions or lack the incentive to get things done.

7 AND 8: You might be dealing with self-doubt, and possibly have low self-esteem or a fear of failure.

9 AND 10: You might struggle to make progress because you lack connection with your future self and overvalue your pleasure in the present.

If you have 4s (often) or 5s (always) for multiple questions, don't worry—there can be more than one reason for procrastinating.

WHAT'S YOUR PROCRASTINATION STYLE?

Although we all put things off, there are seven distinct procrastination types among us. Which one are you? This list can help you zero in on your particular motives for procrastinating. No matter which classification you identify with, try not to feel too badly about it; no reason is worse than any other.

THE AVOIDER

PRONE TO: Avoiding negative emotions or boring tasks.
COULD BE YOU IF: You always switch to easier tasks over challenging ones.

The avoider decides to make the bed when they're supposed to be balancing their checking account. It's a way of running away from stress, anxiety, and other negative feelings. "I just don't feel like it" is a common excuse, as avoiders prioritize their time based on their moods.

THE THRILL-SEEKER

PRONE TO: Leaving today's problem for tomorrow.
COULD BE YOU IF: You do your best work under pressure.

Thrill-seekers live for the pressure of a deadline; they need it to fuel their motivation. Their "I'll just do it later" attitude suggests a lack of connection to their future selves. Procrastination is a way of life, and as a result, things always get done at the last minute, or late.

THE OVERTHINKER

PRONE TO: Feeling overwhelmed and underprepared.
COULD BE YOU IF: You feel like you don't know where to start.

Overthinkers are slow to act because they can't get out of their head or escape their repetitive thoughts. Trapped in the past, they think about negative experiences and blame themselves for previous failures. They get overwhelmed, become over-anxious and indecisive, and place excessive importance on every choice they make.

THE UNDERESTIMATOR

PRONE TO: Making poor decisions based on false assumptions.
COULD BE YOU IF: You often misjudge how much time you need to get something done.

Underestimators mistakenly believe they will have enough time, that the task isn't urgent, that it will be easy, and that everything will be okay. They routinely miss deadlines and often seem disorganized with poor time-management skills . . . though we know that procrastination has deeper causes.

THE PERFECTIONIST

PRONE TO: Fear of failure.

COULD BE YOU IF: You believe that nothing's done until it's perfect.

The perfectionist procrastinates because they're overly committed to doing something "right" or "to perfection." Very critical of themselves, they fear failure and mistakes. They procrastinate when they don't feel ready or able to give their all to a task. They may waste time on unimportant tasks that they could delegate.

THE IMPOSTER

PRONE TO: Self-doubt, low self-esteem, fear of success.

COULD BE YOU IF: It's hard to get started because you feel like a fraud.

The imposter can be held captive not only by self-doubt, but also by fear of being found out. Imposters feel incapable or unworthy; they can't own their accomplishments or abilities. Self-esteem issues put them in an impossible position: if they succeed, they think that it's due to accident, luck, or the efforts of others; if they fail, it confirms what they already knew about themselves. Given that, procrastination feels like the best option.

THE DAYDREAMER

PRONE TO: Dreaming about doing something instead of actually doing it.

COULD BE YOU IF: You dream of success but can't seem to get started.

The daydreamer is afraid that the idea of what they're trying to accomplish is better than accomplishing it, so they don't risk it. Most people actively switch to unimportant tasks when procrastinating; daydreamers do nothing at all, or next to nothing. They tend to occupy themselves with distractions like social media or binge-watching. Their behavior might look like laziness, but it helps them avoid negative emotions and outcomes.

What's Behind the Behavior?

Procrastination is very much a habit. It's an unconscious and automatic response to having to get something done. We've seen that people develop this habit for different reasons and express it in different ways. But in every case, as with all habits, good or bad, procrastination always has a *trigger*. Journalist Charles Duhigg, in his book *The Power of Habit*, explains that all habits have a cue, or trigger, that initiates the routine, which then leads to a reward. For those that procrastinate, the reward is usually an emotional one, a feeling of relief or pleasure at escaping an unpleasant task. But that reward is always temporary.

It's important to understand that one doesn't simply "break" habits. A habit is very deeply wired into your brain, and you can't just switch it off like a light. This is why your previous attempts to stop procrastinating may have failed. A more effective strategy is to *replace* a bad habit with a better, more beneficial one. To do that, you first need to identify your procrastination trigger, that moment that sets you spiraling into inaction. So, let's explore three of the most common triggers for procrastination. No matter what style of procrastination you lean toward, anyone who procrastinates typically struggles with these triggers.

NEGATIVE EMOTIONS

Procrastination is emotional mismanagement, not poor time management. We procrastinate not because of the task itself, but due to our feelings about starting or completing it. As Professor Pychyl puts it: we give up and give in to feel good. This need for instant gratification is seen as a leading cause of procrastination—why feel good later when the task is completed when we can feel good right now by putting it off? Rather than dealing with our negative feelings when they arise, we allow them to trigger our procrastination. The solution to this is establishing healthier and more productive routines for dealing with feelings that arise when we consider the task at hand, such as stress, anxiety, frustration, uneasiness, or even boredom.

Here are some thoughts that tend to arise when we use procrastination to escape negative emotions:

I don't feel like it right now.

I'll do this when I'm in the mood.

I'm too [nervous/distracted/other emotion] right now to do this.

I'll feel like it after I [take a nap/walk the dog/do some other task].

I can't do this; it's going to be [boring/ frustrating/other negative experience].

When you notice thoughts like the ones above, you need to choose a constructive coping mechanism instead of procrastinating. The good news is that in this book we'll build new routines together that can help you work through this discomfort or relieve it entirely, so you can be more productive.

NO PERCEIVED VALUE

Not all triggers are emotional. They can also be based on your values and beliefs, your core convictions about what is right and what is important to you. Our values impact our actions (or in the case of procrastination, our inaction). For example, you may put off your yearly physical exam and dental appointments because you think they are a waste of time and money, but at the same time you keep up the maintenance on your car because you worry about it breaking down.

Psychological studies have shown that people that procrastinate tend to value their present over their future. They take a very "enjoy the now and stress later (if at all)" attitude. The propensity to procrastinate isn't just about the task itself; rather, it is a general overvaluing of present pleasure over future reward. So, whether it's filing taxes, going to an important doctor's appointment, doing chores, or paying a bill on time, people with this type of trigger would rather put off the task and just enjoy life. (One study suggests that some people who procrastinate not only put things off, but they also actually never intend to get them done at all.)

If lack of perceived value is a trigger for you, these thoughts may seem familiar:

I don't even care about this, so why bother?

Getting this done isn't important to me at all.

Who cares? This is just a waste of time.

Forget it. I don't even want to do this.

This doesn't matter anyway.

If you can relate to this kind of thinking, you will need to build habits to help you find value and worth in completing tasks sooner. Not to worry; you'll find out exactly how to do so in this book.

LACK OF INCENTIVE

A reward is a key component of any habit—it's the payoff that makes a habit stick. The same can be said for procrastinating. By putting things off or avoiding them entirely, your "reward" is making you feel better, even if it's just temporary. Which is why it's so tempting to keep procrastinating: it feels good.

Incentives come in two flavors: On one hand are the rewards, things you value or desire that you receive for accomplishing something. But on the other hand are the consequences, which could be negative or harmful results of inaction. Both rewards and consequences work best when they're externally imposed—in other words, when they're not up to you, but designated by someone else. For example, you get promoted for great work or you get fired for slacking off. But in the absence of an external incentive, people with this trigger find themselves thinking:

There's no point getting started on this now.

What's in it for me if I get this done?

I have so much time, I can just do this later.

It's due today, but they don't care if it's in tomorrow.

Why even bother? It will take forever to get this done.

A big problem here is that often an external incentive does exist, but it's so far in the future that it's easily outweighed by the reward of procrastinating. There are no better examples than dieting, exercising, or saving money. If this trigger is familiar to you, keep reading. In this book you'll find out how to create incentives for yourself instead of skipping the race because there's no immediate prize for finishing.

OTHER FACTORS

For some people, procrastination can be rooted in the mood and mental health disorders that they live with every day. Psychologists have linked anxiety, depression, obsessive-compulsive disorder (OCD), attention deficit hyperactivity disorder (ADHD) and similar conditions to procrastination. Here's how these conditions may impact someone's emotional and mental state:

- **ANXIETY DISORDER:** May cause daily intense episodes of fear and worry that can lead to panic attacks.

- **DEPRESSION:** May be felt as extreme sadness, creating a lack of interest in daily life or activities.

- **OBSESSIVE-COMPULSIVE DISORDER (OCD):** Can cause repetitive patterns of irrational thoughts or fears that lead to repetitive behaviors.

- **ATTENTION DEFICIT HYPERACTIVITY DISORDER (ADHD):** Can make it difficult to focus and pay attention.

It's clear how these conditions could impact tendencies to procrastinate. How incredibly challenging would it be to get started on a project or get important tasks done when your emotional and mental state is out of your control? Some experts believe that extreme procrastination might be a sign that someone has one of the conditions listed above. If that applies to you, there's no shame in seeking out professional help and getting the support you need to manage your condition.

Not only can some disorders exacerbate procrastination, but some studies have shown that procrastinating can lead to worsened physical, emotional, and mental states. Yes, you read that correctly: Procrastination is bad for your health. The more you procrastinate, the more you risk your overall health and well-being. You may recall that procrastinating gives you a temporary break from stress and anxiety, but stress and anxiety can worsen in the long run, increasing their unhealthy effects the more you put things off.

The bottom line: Conquering procrastination isn't just about getting stuff done. Intensified stress due to procrastination could impact all aspects of your health. Documented side effects of stress range from high blood pressure, fatigue, and headaches to sadness, anger, and a loss of motivation. By conquering procrastination, you're protecting yourself from its impact on your physical and mental wellness.

How This Book Can Help

With everything you've just learned about procrastination, how it works on a psychological level, and the variations that apply the most to you, you're now ready to face it head-on. You can turn your life around and finally start accomplishing the things that matter to you. I promise you, it's not as scary as it sounds, and I'll be right there with you as you conquer procrastination in every area of your life. No matter your situation—whether you're at home most days, in school, working, or any combination—this book offers real and relatable ideas that you can use.

The chapters ahead are filled with over 30 easy-to-implement strategies that will help you see results. With these tips, tricks, and techniques, I will help you master your to-dos, make maximum use of your time, get motivated, and increase your focus. You'll also discover the power of rewards and incentives, as well as the importance of building momentum. Use this book as your roadmap: Each and every step is important, and together those steps will take you to a productive, procrastination-free future. So, no skipping ahead. Change your procrastination habit one strategy at a time. For best results, take each strategy for a test run after you've learned it and before continuing to the next. Everything you learn along the way will bring you closer to the productive, effective, in-control person you know you can be.

Ready to become your most productive self? Here's a sneak peek at the journey ahead.

TASKS AND GOALS

Chapter 2 will be your foundation for all future strategies, because to conquer procrastination you have to know what needs doing and when it needs to be done. First, you'll kick things off by creating a list of tasks and learn to set goals the SMART way. In this chapter you'll learn how to get your priorities straight so you can rank and rearrange your tasks in order of importance. This is key for managing that familiar feeling of having too much to do and not enough time to do it. By the end of the chapter, you'll know exactly where to start, what to do first, and how to plan ahead.

TIME

We've said that poor time management doesn't cause procrastination. But *effective* time management is a critical tool for conquering procrastination. So, with your tasks, priorities, and goals in order, you'll work toward mastering your time-management skills. You may feel time is the enemy, but it can be your greatest asset if you learn how to make the most of it. The strategies in chapter 3 will show you how to properly use your calendar, implement time blocking, find the right time of day to get to work, and schedule regular breaks. You'll discover how easy it is to get started on your tasks by taking 10-minute baby steps and gain the courage to eat the frog. Eat a frog? You'll have to read the chapter to find out.

MOTIVATION

Motivation is so much more than just a feeling: it's like fuel. To fill your tank, you'll start by discovering your "why," the source of your motivation, and learn how to connect with it daily using visualization. You'll then get creative with a vision board that represents your dreams and goals for the future. Chapter 4 will also teach you to change your inner monologue by embracing the positive. To help get you moving and defying procrastination, you'll learn to make any task into a game. And for those times when you're struggling to get started, you'll bust out your own personal take-action ritual. Never run out of gas again!

FOCUS

It's time to break up with the distractions and interruptions that are robbing you of your productivity. It's time to quit wishing and hoping that you could just stay focused and make it a reality. Whether you're at home, school, work, or out and about, you'll learn how to remove focus-zapping distractions and create the right environment for productivity. Chapter 5 starts by telling you how to create healthy boundaries and balance so you can let others know of your plans and intentions. You'll develop a focused mind through the use of singletasking and become your own motivator, and learn to use a redirecting mantra. Finally, you'll learn when to say no to yourself and to others, protecting your focusing skills going forward in your life.

REWARDS

To stay productive, you need encouragement to be in the game for the long term. If you enjoy treating yourself and claiming rewards—and why wouldn't you?—you'll love the strategies in chapter 6. You'll learn how to savor positive instant gratification, to treat yourself to small luxuries, and to anticipate big indulgences. In this chapter you'll also build a much-needed support system by finding an accountability partner. On the flip side, you'll remind yourself why you're committed to conquering procrastination by acknowledging the very real consequences of your inaction.

LOOKING AHEAD

You're ready to leave procrastination in the rearview mirror as you motor toward a more productive future. But would I send you on your way without some parting gifts? As we end our time together, I'll hand you a final box of tools that will help you maintain what you've gained and keep it moving forward. We'll review the key strategies you've learned, and discuss how to apply them as life throws its challenges and curveballs your way.

To conquer procrastination for now and forever, you need to build momentum. Get started today, begin learning the strategies in the coming chapters, and apply them to your life immediately. Don't wait another day.

WHAT DO YOU VALUE?

Procrastination causes us to ignore the important things we value and the tasks we should prioritize to support those values. Many of us never get started on a task, despite its importance, because we struggle to connect with our future selves and to value the long-term benefit that will come if we put in the effort now. For example, you might say that you value your relationships, health, and financial security. But, the success in each of these areas requires hard work and commitment over time, and the reward isn't always immediate. So, instead of putting money aside for retirement, you spend daily at Starbucks. Or, rather than going to the gym or taking a walk, you drop onto the sofa and watch Netflix.

Before you move on to the next chapter and take control of your tasks and goals, it will be helpful to ask yourself: *What do I value? What matters to me?* The best way to see where your values really lie is to examine how you spend your time, money, and energy. Ideally, you spend more on what you value the most. But as you may see for yourself, that isn't always the case. Consider the following self-reflection questions:

1. What three things do you value the most in life?

2. What do you always have the energy for?

3. How do you use your free time?

4. What do you spend your money on?

Consider your answers. Do the answers to questions 1 through 4 align? Or is there a discrepancy between what you value and what's actually going on in your life?

Do you value making your present easier over your future? Are you present-minded or future-minded? Do you procrastinate completing tasks in the areas you claim to value?

These are hard questions, but you need to be able to answer them. In order to quit procrastinating and direct your efforts toward things that really matter to you, keep your values front-of-mind. Tell yourself why you care about each value. Know the benefits and why they're important to you.

Stop waiting for tomorrow; change the narrative and begin making progress today toward enhancing your values.

CHAPTER 2

Set Your Tasks and Goals

You picked up this book because you want to flip the script, to finally be able to start tasks and carry them through to completion without all the grief and drama. So, it must be time to try and get something important done, right?

Love the enthusiasm, but hold on a second . . . You're missing two key elements. Before you start, you need to set your tasks and identify your goals. Doing so gives you clarity of purpose and the confidence you can do it, as well as a clear starting point.

YES, MAKE A LIST

Let's talk about all those important tasks that you've been putting off. Take a deep breath—for now, we're just discussing why you need a new approach. When you procrastinate, you miss deadlines, lose track of time, run late, miss out on opportunities, and let people down. On the surface, this behavior can look like an organizational and time-management issue, but you and I both know it's an emotional one at its heart.

The truth is, poor organization isn't a cause of procrastination, it's an enabler. People who procrastinate tend to not keep careful track of their obligations and deadlines; if the only place you record them is in your mind, it is even easier to neglect these tasks. So, you keep your tasks and to-dos snuggled up in your memory with all those negative emotions you're trying to avoid. It's like a game in there, with thoughts of getting things done popping up and immediately being consumed by anxiety or stress. Eventually time runs out, and it's game over.

Let There Be Lists

The simplest step toward conquering your procrastination can be summed up in four words: Write. It. All. Down. You need to make a list (and check it at least twice, but more on that later). Before you even go there, I know what you're thinking: *I have a great memory. I know what I need to do, I don't need to write things down.* Nice try, friend, but you do. Here's why: When you write something down, you begin to declutter your mind. You make space in your brain's hard drive by downloading a bit of information to external storage. And with that load lightened, you feel less overwhelmed.

Making your master list of the things you need to do initiates an encouraging dialogue with yourself. With each new item you add, you acknowledge that task's importance and set your intention to do it. This is vital—you're now taking that task more seriously than you did when it was one thought, among many, in your head. You're telling yourself that this task is of value—yes, it's worthy of your time and effort.

List Time, Write Now

Now, let's make that list. Be sure to not skip this step, as you'll be using your master list of tasks to explore all the strategies in this chapter. Use whatever form of documentation you prefer—a blank sheet of paper, a favorite notebook, a brand-new journal, or even a new doc on your mobile device if that's how you roll. Write down everything you need to do. Everything. *Everything.* Don't hold back, don't leave things out, and don't dismiss anything. Even if a task doesn't feel that important at the moment, it came to mind for a reason, so jot it down. There's no right number of tasks to write down; draft a list right now that's as close to complete as you can make it.

Take your time. To help you brain dump all your tasks, chores, obligations, and projects, consider these reflection questions:

» What do you need to get done?

» Is there anything you've been avoiding?

» Are any tasks keeping you up at night?

» Is anything due soon or overdue?

» What have you forgotten about?

It can also help to review the What Do You Value? exercise in chapter 1 (page 20). Connecting with what's valuable to you might shake loose some important business that needs your attention.

I know firsthand the power of writing things down and collecting my thoughts. For me, this practice started as a post-vacation ritual. Picture me sitting in an airport, laptop open, typing out my to-do list. With every line, my anxiety about returning to the real world lifted a little. Here's a look at my current list, in no particular order:

» Clean out the basement

» Get an oil change

» Go to the dentist

- » File my taxes

- » Finish writing chapter 2

- » And so much more

The point of this exercise is to pull everything from your mind and put it where you can see it. It's hard to miss that master list when its sitting on your desk, in your planner, on your computer, or even posted on your fridge. Bonus points for using pen and paper; physically writing something down has been proven to help you remember it.

Done making your list? If you think so, then you are. With your list of tasks in hand, you'll be able to find a starting place. To do that, we're going to prioritize, make a plan, and even set some goals. The list you just made is your jumping off point, so get ready.

GET YOUR PRIORITIES STRAIGHT

With your master list of tasks written out, you might find yourself staring at this to-do document and feeling overwhelmed again. But there's no cause for concern. Because guess what? You're about to discover an amazing truth: *You don't need to do everything.* That's right. You may have been procrastinating things that didn't need to be procrastinated. It sure feels good to check something off your to-do list, but it's even better to realize you don't need to do that task at all. And that's the significance of prioritizing: without clear priorities, everything can feel important, even the things that don't matter.

Before you can prioritize the tasks on your master list, you need to know what your priorities are. Did you catch that? You need priorities to prioritize. Here's why: A lack of clear priorities can lead to indecision and inaction, two procrastination hallmarks.

What Comes First?

Only you can determine your priorities, but to help you figure it out, review the following list of general concerns that most people have. They're listed in no special order. If any of the items below resonate with you on a deep level, you can add a checkmark beside it or even rank the priorities in order of relevance. Turn back to the What Do You Value? exercise (page 20) to remind yourself of what's most important to you. Some common priorities in your life might be:

» Family and friends

» Career and work

» Education and learning

» Helping and giving back

» Fun and enjoyment

» Health and fitness

» Money and finances

» Faith and spirituality

» Travel and adventure

Which of these examples is most in line with your priorities? It's okay if what you're thinking about isn't on this list. These are very general categories, and your priorities might be more specific. For example, my priorities in life right now are financial freedom and getting healthier. Knowing this helps me to prioritize my three main resources in life: my time, my money, and my energy.

Still not quite sure what your priorities might be? Use the following reflection questions to get your priorities straight:

» What matters the most to you right now?

» What areas of your life do you want to improve?

» What's critical or essential to your future?

» What have you been neglecting?

These questions might seem vague at first, but if you read through them a few times, honest answers will follow. For some, this might be an eye-opening process. You might feel sad, guilty, or even ashamed about putting off your priorities. Don't hold on to those feelings. Be proud that you're working on this now, because this is important. You know all too well that you only have so much to give each day, especially when you take into account all your other responsibilities, from work or school to home life and relationships. Having priorities helps you focus your remaining resources on what's most important to you. (Sorry, but unless you're a TV blogger, binge-watching TV shouldn't be ranked number one on your list of priorities.)

Are your priorities clearer now? I sure hope so.

Priority Pitfalls

Here are three snares that might trip you up as you evaluate your priorities, and suggestions on how to unsnag yourself:

Second-guessing your choices. I want you to always remember this; read it twice if you have to: Whatever you decide your priorities are, whatever it is that you deem worthy of your time, money, and energy, *own it*. Know that it's the right choice for you, trust your instincts, and don't allow yourself to overthink it. Overthinking is just procrastination's cousin, and you need to break up with that, too.

Losing sight of why. Be sure to keep your eyes on the prize, especially if this process is a struggle. Remind yourself that getting your priorities straight clears the fog and helps you know with certainty where you need to focus your attention. You'll need that conviction, that commitment, to help you get started and get things done. It takes strong resolve to resist the urge to procrastinate. I want you to have that.

Fear of missing out. You might feel a fear of missing out if you prioritize, since placing importance on one thing inevitably means putting less importance onto something else. As the famous saying goes, "You can have it all. You just can't have it all at once."

The reality is that you can't do everything now, but by prioritizing, you'll be able to do more later.

SET A GOAL, MAKE IT SMART

If you have no idea where you're going, it's hard to know what route to take, or even which direction to move in, and you could end up driving in circles. That's why setting goals is a such powerful strategy for combating procrastination. It's easy to put something off when you're not going anywhere. But a target in your sights puts you in the driver's seat. Goal-setting provides the practical and motivational push you need: it helps you figure out what you need to do—your target—as well as giving you the desire to do it.

Why Setting a Goal Matters

Have you ever had to do something just for the sake of getting it done? A task or project can feel pretty pointless without a goal to give your actions greater purpose and meaning. That's why any good weight loss program starts with goal-setting; if somebody has a reason to get in shape, they're more likely to succeed. Someone might want to lose weight to be more confident, to be happier with themselves, to correct health problems, or even just to fit in those jeans from 10 years ago.

Similarly, you need a reason to conquer procrastination. So, what is procrastination keeping you from achieving or experiencing? Think about that. Feel free to get upset or even mad about it. No judgement—any reason will do as long as it's honest. What's your goal? Where do you want to be? What are you working toward? Where will conquering your procrastination get you? Just as with your list of tasks, writing down your goals is a critical step for success. One goal-setting study, conducted by psychologist Gail Matthews, PhD, at Dominican University of California, revealed that those who wrote down their goals were 30 percent more likely to succeed than those who didn't. I don't know about you, but I want the odds on my side. Here's a format you can use to craft a goal statement, and some simple examples to get you thinking:

I want to conquer procrastination because . . .

» *I'm tired of my life being on hold.*

» *I'm done waiting, I want to start living.*

» *I'm ready to get healthy and fit.*

» *I just want to be happy and love my life.*

» *I want to be debt-free with financial security.*

» *I'd love to spend time on the things that matter most* (see What Do You Value? page 20).

It's Smart to Be SMART

If you want even better odds of success, you'll make sure your goal is SMART: Specific, Measurable, Achievable, Relevant, and Timely. This is the gold standard for goal-setting, creating an objective that not only determines your destination but also defines why it's important, and how and when you'll achieve it. Creating a SMART goal is a boss move and will help you kick procrastination-triggering doubting thoughts to the curb.

Take a look at the goal statement you wrote out earlier. Revise it as needed until it meets the SMART guidelines by answering the questions below.

S: What SPECIFICALLY will you achieve?

M: How can you MEASURE your success?

A: How will you ACHIEVE your goal?

R: How is this goal RELEVANT to you?

T: What's your TIMELINE?

Here's a pro-tip: If your goal uses adjectives like "happy," "healthy," or any other unclear "feels good but doesn't really mean anything" words, then specify what they mean. Like this:

ORIGINAL GOAL: Get healthy

SMART GOAL STATEMENT: My goal is to lose 15 pounds. (S) and be fit enough to run the local 5K (M) next summer (T) by working out three times a week and changing what I eat (A). I'm in pain every day from my desk job and need to get stronger more than anything (R).

ORIGINAL GOAL: Be happy

SMART GOAL STATEMENT: I feel disconnected from who I really am (R). I want to have time for my hobbies (S) and spend a few hours (M) one evening a week (T) on them by reorganizing my schedule and clearing commitments (A).

Can you see the difference? Having a SMART goal adds several layers of clarity. Equipped with this knowledge, you'll find it even easier to weed out the not-so-important tasks from your master list. Plus, who doesn't love having a sense of purpose, excitement, and urgency?

RANK AND REARRANGE

Here we go. You're about to get a handle on your master list and take back your life. For too long, procrastination has taken control of your time, but not after this moment. And for dramatic effect, you could even work on this strategy using a red pen. Somehow, I find that it's more empowering that way.

Okay, let's attack that master list: all the things you want, need, and should be doing. With your priorities now in line, and your goals firmly in mind (and on paper), it's time to rank and rearrange your master list so you can find your starting point.

Important, Urgent, Both, or Neither?

For this strategy, we're turning to one of the most productive people in history for help: President Dwight D. Eisenhower. You're going to use a simplified version of his method, the Eisenhower Matrix (see the Resources section for more), for prioritizing tasks, namely sorting them according to two important qualities:

IMPORTANCE: A task is *important* when it's an essential step toward something you need or want to achieve, like your SMART goal. For example, if your goal is to pay off your debts, important steps might be cutting spending and creating a budget.

URGENCY: A task is *urgent* when it's time-sensitive and must be done immediately. Continuing with our example, an urgent task would be paying your credit card's monthly minimum payment to avoid a penalty or going to your appointment with a debt consolidation specialist.

So, let's apply those designations to the tasks on your master list. Using your goals and priorities to help you, assign a number to each task, from 1 to 4, as described below. We're sorting every single thing on your to-do list into the following four categories, which will determine how you handle those tasks.

CATEGORY 4: **Delete It.** These are tasks that are *neither important nor urgent*. Being nonessential, they're "would be nice" to-dos, activities you would pursue if you had resources to spare. Any task that does not support your priorities or your goals belongs here. For example, if your number-one priority is cutting your spending, you'd have to move "renovating the kitchen" into this category. I know it's hard, but remember you can't do it all right now. Mark these tasks with a 4, to revisit them someday, or cross them off your list for good (this can be so satisfying).

CATEGORY 3: **Delegate It.** Tasks on your list that are *urgent but not important* get marked with a 3. You want these done on time, but don't need to do them yourself—which brings up an essential principle in conquering procrastination: Whether you're at work, at school, or at home, it's important to be supported by others. Perhaps you have an assistant or colleague at work who can take something off your plate. Maybe your kids are old enough to start doing some cleaning chores. In fact, with so many apps and online services, you can delegate almost anything these days (see the Resources list at the end of the book).

CATEGORY 2: **Do It Later.** All the remaining items on your master list need to be done; it's just a question of whether to tackle them sooner or later. In this category, we have stuff you're allowed to "procrastinate." Just kidding, of course—you're prioritizing, not procrastinating. Yes, you need to get these done. However, these tasks are *important but not urgent*, so there's no rush. Here's an example: You're a college student, and your list is filled with assignments, exams, classes, cleaning, and the like. Everything that isn't due in the next few days to one week would belong here. Use the number 2 to rank these kinds of tasks for later.

CATEGORY 1: **Do It Now.** The remaining tasks on your master list should qualify as *both important and urgent*. That means they all need to get done right away. The urgency could come from a deadline, a penalty for lateness, a scheduled appointment, or even a promise to someone else. This includes any emergencies as well. At the very top would be any fires you need to put out now. For example, seeing a doctor about a medical condition, paying your rent or mortgage, or studying for an exam you have tomorrow. These must-dos are just the sort of tasks that procrastination causes you to avoid and ignore.

Remember when you first created your master list, and it was a jumble of tasks all mixed together like the stuff in a kitchen junk drawer? Those days are gone, friend. Now everything is organized and in separate bins. And you can see exactly which tasks to grab hold of first.

SET DAILY MUST-DOS

Every single day, you wake up with the opportunity to be productive and get things done. And when you make use of that opportunity, you can go to bed with a smile on your tired face, because you know you did everything you could. Every productive day starts the moment you get out of bed. And the surefire way to set up your day for success is to set your daily must-do list.

A must-do list is a more focused, more intentional excerpt of a master list. Maybe you've tried making a list like this before, only to leave the house with a superlong inventory that felt impossible to complete in a single day. That was then, and this is now. At this point, you're ahead of the game with your master list ranked by level of necessity, and you know what needs to get done first.

How Many Must-Dos Must I Do?

The point is not to do as many tasks as you can each day. Rather, your mission is to get the most *critical* task(s) done. How long that list will be is going to vary from person to person. It depends entirely on how much time you have to dedicate to them. So, please be realistic when you set yours, especially at the start. There's no need to get overwhelmed or try to overdo it. For example, if you work 9-to-5 and have family or other after-work commitments, perhaps all you can manage is one small task a day. But on the other hand, if you're self-employed and your tasks relate to your business, then you can most likely manage more. In either case, you're increasing your productivity by applying yourself to the task that will have the biggest impact.

So, how many must-dos should you have? A good rule of thumb is to start with one per day if your time is limited, and at most, pick three. If you're unable to complete your must-dos for one day, no worries at all—don't feel bad, just carry them over into the next day. The effect of your must-do list on your morale is cumulative; each day you'll see at least one important task completed. As you build your confidence, you can try taking on more. But avoid overloading. In the beginning, less is best.

To create your must-do list, pull the top-priority and emergency-level tasks from your master list—anything that simply cannot wait: category 1 tasks for sure, and if there's room, the most important of category 2. (As a best practice, whenever you finish the day's must-dos, consider if there's time to start on any category 2 tasks, before they escalate into something urgent.) Your method for recording your must-do list doesn't have to be anything fancy. A note on your mirror, an entry in your day planner, or a piece of paper left on the kitchen table will work perfectly.

To help increase your focus, try writing your lists out the night before, noting the tasks you'll do tomorrow and the next day. This way, you can hit the ground running every morning. The only real rule for your must-do list is to always keep it simple and small. You do not want to trigger your procrastination with an overwhelming list of tasks. This is why you'll be referring to your must-do list on a daily basis, not your master list of tasks.

Examples of Daily Must-Dos

Here are some examples of setting 1 to 3 daily must-dos:

Must-dos for a busy parent might be:

» Sign the kids up for an after-school program.

» Bake cookies for tomorrow's bake sale.

» Pay the electricity bill.

Must-dos for someone in the corporate world might consist of:

» Finish the quarterly report.

» Submit my self-assessment.

» Check in with my team members.

Must-dos for a college student might be:

» Study for Friday's biology exam.

» Send in financial aid forms.

Must-dos for after work could include:

» Book a dentist appointment.

My own must-do list for any given day usually has just a few tasks: replying to emails, paying invoices, drafting a blog post. Once you become a master at checking off your daily tasks, you can even start adding some "if there's time" tasks to your list.

After writing your list, keep it where you can see it and refer back to it throughout the day. No questions about what you should do today, and no anxiety about tomorrow to keep you up all night. It's a win-win situation.

ALWAYS PLAN AHEAD

Now that you're managing your daily must-dos, let's take a longer view and plan ahead. This way, you won't have any surprises, shocks, or setbacks. Instead, you'll enjoy the peace of mind that comes from knowing exactly what you need to do and when. With your highest-priority tasks tracked on your must-do list, you can prepare for your category 2 "do it later" tasks. I know it's tempting to continue to put these tasks off, to avoid getting started until they enter the danger zone. But doing so would just reinforce procrastination. You've decided that these tasks are important—they're in line with your goals and values—and you don't want to wait until they're all urgent. To handle those as soon as you're able, you need to plan ahead.

Here are a few situations where procrastination could be averted by planning ahead:

» How many times have you woken up in the morning unsure about what to wear, then wasted time trying on too many things and ended up late for work?

» Have you ever come home without a plan for what to do after work and ended up in front of the TV for hours? Watching something you don't even like?

» You're going out, but you haven't specified an exact time to leave, so you decide to check your email for a few minutes and end up being late even though you had plenty of time.

Without planning ahead, you're inviting procrastination to the party. In these everyday situations, procrastination is like a fog that expands to fill any void in your schedule left by your indecisiveness and lack of preparation. Before you know it, you've forgotten all about what you need to do. Time is precious, so stop putting it at risk.

Plan for "Later" Now

With a process in place for your top-priority to-dos, it's time to rank your remaining category 2 tasks in order of potential urgency. What needs to get done first? And then after that? Essentially, you're answering the question "what's next?" And in the absence of any actual deadlines for these tasks, you'll need to set them for yourself so you have enough time to accomplish them.

Referring to your master list, write out any remaining important but not urgent tasks (category 2). For each task, assign a realistic start date and completion date, taking into consideration how long it will take to complete the task.

How does that work exactly? Well, for each task, ask yourself *How much time do I need to do this?* Then, look at your answer, and ask *Realistically, how much?* If you're not sure, think about similar tasks you've completed before. How long did they take? Or, ask a friend or colleague what to expect. You can also turn to your search engine of choice, asking, "How long does it take to [insert task here]." Note these time requirements beside each task. Decide when you want or need to have the task done and work backward to find a realistic start date.

For example:

» **Write a 3,000-word paper on the economics of middle America.** You know that it takes one day to research and take notes, another one to two evenings in the library to write your draft and the last to edit. *Four days to complete. Due Nov. 29. Start Nov. 25 or sooner.*

» **Hire an electrician to replace the kitchen light before my mother visits.** You assume it'll take a day or two to find someone to hire, another to grab the new light fixture from the store, and then you'll be waiting for the installation date. *Two weeks to complete. Due March 25. Start by March 10.*

» **Find a new job that pays better.** The last time you went job hunting, it took six months to land a position. You're more connected in your industry now and have a recruiter, so you estimate it should take a few months. *Four months to complete. Want to be done by summer. Start in February.*

An added benefit of planning ahead is that you're shifting your mindset from your present to your future—thus, being more compassionate and caring toward your future self. You can see from each of these examples that you can't properly accomplish any of these tasks at the last minute. If you find yourself thinking otherwise about a task, pay attention to what might be holding you back. Frankly, it sounds a lot like putting things off that you could do sooner. When you're tempted to avoid planning your do-later tasks, picture yourself calm and collected, waking up every day knowing what needs to get done that day, that week, and that month, and not giving procrastination a chance to step in.

CHAPTER 3

Get Time on Your Side

Productivity and time management: They're often discussed together and sometimes even mistaken for one another. They're besties, a power couple who work together to help you get things finished on time. You need both of them on your side, because with their assistance you'll be able to get the job done sooner, faster, and more efficiently.

So, let's talk about time. When you procrastinate, it can feel as if time is your enemy: chasing you down, always running out before you're finished. But is that really what's happening? If anything, it's time who should be complaining about us. When we put things off, it's easy to lose track of time, neglecting it like that friend we should talk to but never do. No wonder time's not there when we need it. But with the following time-management techniques, you can repair your dysfunctional relationship with time, make it your buddy again, and get time on your side. And when time's your bud, time's good friend productivity comes along. Isn't that great?

USE YOUR CALENDAR

No time-management tool is more important than a calendar. Without it, there isn't much you can do in this department; with it, the world is your well-scheduled oyster. There are plenty to choose from; calendars are everywhere. Almost everyone has a smartphone, tablet, or computer, and they all come with a calendar installed. If you prefer to work with an old-school physical calendar, there's no need to buy one, as many local businesses offer them for free. I'd be completely lost without the perfectly sized desk calendar from my local bank.

Calendars to Consider

In fact, a paper or other physical calendar is a good choice even if you're leading a mostly electronic lifestyle. Yes, you usually carry your device with you at all times, which is a plus. But there's something about physically writing out your plans that makes them stick. Plus, it's easier to ignore an app on your phone than the planner on your desk or the calendar hanging on the wall (especially if it has pictures of puppies on it). On the other hand, digital calendars have some pretty useful bells and whistles that act as reminders. This is why I encourage you to use a physical calendar as well as a digital one. Here are four types of calendars to pair with your digital device of choice.

> » PAPER CALENDAR: Available anywhere and sometimes even for free. Pick one up at your local bank, grocer, or bookshop. These are great for under-estimators and thrill-seekers who benefit from seeing how much time they have.

> » DAY PLANNER: The perfect choice for overthinkers and anyone who needs the space to think through all the steps on paper. Since they're small, you can keep them with you.

> » PRINTABLE CALENDAR: Printables offer anyone with easy access to a printer the ability to reuse pages as many times as

they like and the flexibility to customize and be creative. Search online for a free or cheap one.

» **ERASABLE WALL CALENDAR:** Varying in size, mountable wall calendars with dry erase markers are potentially the most expensive choice. Easy to update and revise, they're hard to miss, so they're good daily reminders for avoiders. The only disadvantage is that they require monthly updating.

Fill 'er Up!

A calendar is like a coloring book, made to be filled in. Here's how to put your calendar to good use:

Mark the days. Use your calendar to track your personal and professional life. Add all your dates: appointments, due dates, deadlines, meetings, parties, trips, birthdays, vacations, and events. To ensure that you get things done and are prepared for upcoming events, set alerts on your digital calendar so you have time to get started.

You don't need to add absolutely everything to your calendar, just anything that's irregular and important. For example, if you have the same work schedule every single week or if you drop the kids off every day at the same time, you may not need these on your calendar. On the other hand, you will want to add changes in your class schedule or any extra shifts you pick up at work.

Share your schedule. If you share a calendar, be sure to make full use of it by adding events, appointments, and any timely information. This will not only get you organized but also keep everyone else in your life informed and hopefully cut down on requests for your time when you're booked up. If your work group uses a shared calendar, keep it up to date and reserve time for working uninterrupted, as well as for breaks and meetings. Free digital calendars make it easy to collaborate and share calendars with family members, house-mates, book clubs, and other groups. By sharing your schedule you're also sharing your deadlines, which adds some much-needed accountability (more on this later).

Add your to-dos. Once your calendar is filled with all your commitments, you can decide on dates and times to work on your must-do tasks. If possible, choose the same day and time on a weekly basis, like Tuesdays after class or Fridays when the kids are at school. Choosing a set time will build a habit of utilizing this time to get things done. When you write your to-dos, check your well-documented paper calendar and schedule the time. Don't forget to set reminders and notify your shared digital calendar that you'll be busy. Take your top priorities as seriously as a work shift or important appointment.

TAKE 10-MINUTE BABY STEPS

Even if it's on our must-do list, when a task feels tedious, too big, or seems like it could take forever, our response might be to put it off. We often find ourselves thinking, *This isn't the right time,* or *I don't have enough time for this today.* But these kinds of thoughts buy into the perfectionist fairy tale that conditions must be "perfect" for you to begin. At the root of these beliefs is a false perception of time—specifically, that you need some minimum amount of it available in order to be productive. Whether or not you're aware of it, this all-or-nothing attitude is feeding your procrastination and keeping you from making progress.

You need to break free of this unrealistic belief, and here's why: Productivity is not an all-or-nothing proposition. Every little bit counts, and even teeny, tiny steps matter. Stop believing the lie. Right now, at this very moment, whatever else is going on in your life, you have enough time to get started on whatever you want to do. And I know it might not feel that way, but the strategy I'm about to share will make a believer out of you. Trust me, I get it. I used to feel that unless I could do it all, be 100 percent in, somehow my efforts didn't count and they weren't good enough. But they are. Every baby step counts.

Examples of Baby Steps

Rarely, if ever, can you get it all done at once. Life is a marathon, not a sprint; it's a series of small steps. Making progress over time makes you a winner. If you've ever wanted to save money, you know that you have to save in increments. To save $1,000, you first have to be able to put aside $10, then $10 more, and so on. If you want to get healthy, you make small healthy choices over and over again: drinking more water, exercising, becoming more active, eating healthier meals. All these baby steps more than add up in the end.

Here are even more examples of 10-minute baby steps for a variety of goals and tasks:

» Need to clean your house? Sweep or vacuum the floors.

» Have to organize your closet? Clean out one drawer.

» Have to file your taxes? Collect your receipts and records.

» Putting off writing a paper? Brainstorm some ideas.

» Too many emails needing replies? Respond to two or three of them.

» Want to get out of debt? Find two items at home that you can sell online.

» Have a report due at work? Create an outline.

What baby steps can you take? Start with your must-do list, as it contains your most important and urgent tasks. Break down the very first task you need to accomplish into simple baby steps.

The Baby Step Mindset

Now, it's your turn to take your very first baby step. You need to find just 10 undistracted minutes you can dedicate to getting something done. Don't overthink it—just decide and do it. Speak to yourself encouragingly, with phrases like, *I can do this now*, *I've got this*, and *I can do 10 minutes*. With this small amount of time, you begin to build confidence and prove to yourself that you can beat procrastination, 10 minutes at a time. Isn't this sense of accomplishment amazing? Then repeat, committing yourself to another 10-minute step. You'll soon begin to see even the most complicated tasks as tiny, bite-size bits. What used to overwhelm you now feels more than manageable.

An added benefit of taking baby steps is that with each successful step, you become increasingly aware of how many 10-minute time chunks are available to you. Every day is filled with opportunities to get ahead, from the last 10 minutes of your lunch break to time spent in the car waiting for the kids to finish soccer practice. Rather than filling these gaps with idle tasks like checking social media, the possibility of taking another 10-minute baby step will begin to excite you. Before you know it, taking a 10-minute step will be easy. You may even find yourself taking 20-minute or longer steps.

TIME BLOCKING, NOT MULTITASKING

Ready to graduate from baby steps and dedicate yourself to more than 10 minutes at a time? You might assume that committing to more time will enable you to accomplish more; that more time equals more progress. Ah, if only time management always translated into productivity that simply. For this equation to work, you need to break one of the modern age's most common bad habits: multitasking.

Don't feel too bad about your multitasking tendencies. This practice is often praised by busy people trying to get lots of things done at the same time. Multitasking is that thing you do almost every day that you swear is your superpower. Actually, it's the opposite, and multiple scientific studies agree: Multitasking is not great for productivity or for your brain. Multitasking has been linked to increased distraction and mental health issues (like stress, anxiety, and depression), reduced brain function and performance, and so many other unproductive side effects. I'm sorry to say that instead of juggling multiple tasks well, you're quite possibly doing them all poorly. I'll go so far as to ask, could your multitasking addiction be procrastination in disguise? It very well might be.

Singletasking is the New Multitasking

I know, the thought of not checking your email while also writing a shopping list and organizing your sock drawer is giving you the heebie-jeebies. What are you supposed to do? How do you manage all the things you need to do while maximizing your time? The answer is simple: *singletask*. Instead of juggling multiple things at the same time, you'll focus on them one at a time. When you're singletasking, your efficiency increases because you get better and faster as time goes on—instead of slower and less focused as you switch between tasks.

The best way to create focused times for singletasking is with a strategy called "time blocking." It's exactly what it sounds like: You block off dedicated time for a single task or a series of similar tasks. For example, if you have must-dos that require your computer, or you need to pay all your bills, do them all at once. Similarly, if you have errands to run in the city center or shopping to do at multiple stores, get them done together. Another great candidate for time blocking is weekly meal prep. Baby steps get you started on your tasks; time blocking helps you make progress more quickly by eliminating the multitasking mindset.

How to Time Block

Here's where your digital calendar shines: Open it to a full week view. Referring to your list of must-dos, determine which tasks require a solid block of time to complete and which ones you can group together. (You can use a day planner for this or print out a weekly calendar to fill in by hand; just follow the same steps.) Now start blocking. Each block is a stretch of time in your schedule devoted to a task or series of tasks. Blocks of 30 minutes to an hour are a good start, but you can try shorter ones if that's all your schedule can handle. Don't overdo it and exhaust yourself with longer time periods. And include a 5- to 10-minute break in the middle of a long block. (We'll talk more about taking breaks soon.)

Your time blocks are reserved for the *designated tasks only*. They're as important as a doctor's appointment, work meeting, or any other event on your schedule. The fantastic part about using time blocks is that as you do it, you start to create a productive routine for yourself. Remember, conquering procrastination requires replacing this habit with one that helps you focus, gets you started, and accomplishes tasks. Time blocking is the productive, positive habit that is going to replace procrastination. When a task evokes feelings of anxiety, boredom, or self-doubt, reach for your calendar. As you start using time blocking, think about what periods of time are available each week for getting things done. Whenever you do so, time blocking becomes a stronger response, an easier choice to make than procrastination. You're training yourself to be more productive.

FIND THE RIGHT TIME OF DAY

Can we talk about the sleeping elephant in the room? Do you ever have those times in an ordinary day when, despite your best intentions, you just suddenly feel tired and maybe a bit lazy? In those moments of low energy, you may procrastinate because it's so easy. You know better, but doing nothing, avoiding any activity of importance, is the most comfortable choice. If this feels familiar, don't worry, you're not alone. Our energy level plays a huge part in our ability to be productive. And nobody operates at full steam all the time. It's hard to resist your procrastination tendencies when you're running on fumes. So, what's the solution?

This is why we simply cannot discuss time management without discussing energy management. Not your electricity bill—you've got that on your calendar now, so I'm not worried about it. Rather, we're talking about your personal energy level, which naturally fluctuates throughout the day. Everyone has unique peak, medium, and low times during any given day that are influenced by their sleep patterns and other factors. Generally speaking, most people tend to be either an early bird or a night owl. Early birds are morning people, most energetic in the early hours of the day. Night owls start slow and become more energized in the later parts of the day and evening. Do you know which one you are? Think about a typical day for you, and note the hours when you do your best work.

Be an Energy Detective

Would it be easier for you to get things done when you're wide awake or when you're dragging at the end of the day and ready for bed? This is not a trick question, I promise. The answer should be rather obvious, yet how many of us try to check things off our to-do lists when we've already used up most of the day's energy? How many of us use energy bars or drinks and way too much caffeine to give us a boost when our energy level has petered out? Here's an example: You're an early bird whose energy peaks at 10:00 a.m. and then again at 1:00 p.m. But you leave important tasks for after dinner, when you barely have the energy to watch TV, and you end up procrastinating because it's just too hard to get going at that hour. Your tank is out of gas, so it's no wonder you stall out.

By managing your energy, and not just your time, you're able to get more done with less effort. No more struggling to build up the energy by slapping water on your face, jumping up and down, and throwing back three espresso shots. Instead of fighting your natural energy rhythm, use it to your advantage. Pay attention throughout the day and note when you're best able to be productive, and then start scheduling important tasks at those times.

Use a notebook, spreadsheet, or even the notes app on your mobile phone to keep a record of energy levels. Be a detective by tracking your energy throughout the day using words like "boost" or "spike" when you feel energized, or "drop" and "dip" for when your energy falls. Make note of the times you get the most done or accomplish a big task. Here's an example of what I mean:

MONDAY: 8:00 a.m. wake up; 10:00 a.m. energy boost, finished paperwork; 12:00 p.m. drop and lunch; then 2:00 p.m. spike, completed report; 4:00 p.m. dinner, energy drop.

FRIDAY: 9:00 a.m. wake up, really low-energy until afternoon and evening; boost around 5:00 p.m. to finish housework and chores; another spike around 8:00 p.m. to finish work.

Track your energy levels for several days or even a week, so you can see the patterns. Then analyze the results: Make a document with three columns, labeled high, medium, and low energy. Fill in the columns with the times of day from your notes. Then use those times accordingly:

HIGH-ENERGY: Keep this time reserved for your most challenging—and most important—tasks.

MEDIUM-ENERGY: Use this slot for tasks that don't require as much brainpower and effort.

LOW-ENERGY: This is your time to rest, relax, and recharge, not a productive time to work.

Using your energy schedule, you can achieve more with a 10-minute baby step at a high-energy time than an hour-long time block during a low-energy time. And I'd be remiss not to remind you that healthy habits will boost your energy levels; getting enough sleep and hydration throughout the day, regular exercise, and eating a healthy diet will show in your energy levels.

DO THE HARD THING FIRST

What's the first that thing you accomplish every day? Would you say it's usually the easiest item on the day's agenda or the most challenging? It's tempting to give yourself a warm-up period and ease into difficult tasks. But to secure your daily productivity, you need to turn that practice on its head and complete the hardest, most important task before anything else. On any given day, "hardest" may mean something different. It might be something that's difficult to complete or the most joyless, unappealing, uninteresting, and tedious task on your list. It's that thing you need to dig deep and almost force yourself to do. The task you're sweating over, or even dreading, because it brings up all those procrastination-feeding emotions? That's the one. Completing the most difficult task first allows you to tackle it when you're most rested and ready. Ideally, that's as early in your day as possible. (Extreme night owls, you might want to wait until later in the day. But maybe not; keep reading because there's more to the story.)

This strategy is not just a matter of expending energy before it's used on other things. Getting the hardest part out of the way allows you to move forward, knowing that things will only get better from here. As the popular saying goes, if you have to eat a live frog, do it first thing in the morning, and most likely nothing worse will happen the rest of the day. Since you're already creating your daily must-do lists the night before, it's easy to decide which tasks to start with. You can even tell yourself, *First thing tomorrow, I'm going to [insert top task here],* or *I will get [project] done as soon as I'm up.* This positive reinforcement goes a long way to building your confidence and courage to just get it done.

Just Do It

Tackling the hardest task first goes against the grain for many of us, but it's a very powerful strategy. Imagine for a moment how vastly different your day would be with the most difficult thing out of the way. You won't have the thoughts, fears, stress, and anxiety of this "super important" task running wild in your mind all day long. Instead of avoiding it until the last minute, you've taken this massive weight off your shoulders. In the absence of that big bad wolf of a task, everything else looks so much more approachable and doable. If you survive the hardest, you'll thrive on the easiest. The rest of your hours are left for the "not so bad," and even enjoyable, tasks.

And here's another reason to take on the most difficult to-dos first: You can't control other people, and you can't stop the chaos of everyday life. Get that chore out of the way and then, even if something urgent and unexpected comes out of nowhere, or life gets in the way as it always does, you're good. You got it done. This strategy protects you from procrastination, distractions, and interruptions outside of your immediate control. Your boss might assign an urgent task, your child could get sick, your Internet connection might cut out, your housemates could come home and make a ruckus. It won't matter. Things happen, and they always will, but you can limit their impact on your productivity if you're ahead of the game.

TAKE SCHEDULED BREAKS

What? Take a break? This might seem counterintuitive in a discussion about productivity, but it really isn't. Taking scheduled breaks throughout the day actually keeps you productive. Here's why: Your brain simply cannot stay focused for a long time, working nonstop on a single task. If you've ever pushed yourself too far in one go, trying to power through a monster task without stopping, you know that once the time clicks past a certain point, it becomes a real struggle to keep going. Your mind turns to mush. You can force yourself to stay at your desk or keep crunching numbers, but your productivity drops to zero. By trying to do too much without resting, you lose focus and the quality of your work slips.

A subtler version of that effect happens even sooner than you think, slowing you down when you don't realize it. To prevent this drop in productivity, you need to regularly stop and step away. I promise, it's not cheating; there are very real limits to your concentration. And the science agrees; multiple studies conclude that taking breaks increases mental agility. The suggested ratio is around one 15- to 20-minute break for every 50 to 60 minutes of work. On the extreme end, those breaks could be every 90 minutes, depending on the task and energy required to accomplish it. So, are you taking enough breaks? Probably not.

Those of us who do take breaks are more creative, have better memory, are healthier, more motivated, stay energized, and are better able to deal with emotional and mental issues like anxiety. Remember those unfriendly emotions you've been avoiding by procrastinating? Taking breaks offers a solution that doesn't hurt your productivity. It keeps you fresh and focused and helps you maintain your energy and excitement levels throughout the day.

Use the Pomodoro Technique

Taking breaks is a smart way to manage your time, as well as sustain your productivity. The key is to ensure that your breaks are sandwiched by productive bursts, like a tasty slice of tomato between two crunchy lettuce leaves. For example, you might work for 20 minutes, take a 3-minute break, work for 45 minutes, then take a 10-minute break. The length of both depends entirely on the task and what works best for you. A popular way to structure breaks is by using the Pomodoro Technique. Developed in the 1980s by business consultant Francesco Cirillo, this time-management system sets 25-minute work sessions known as "Pomodoros," followed by 5-minute breaks. They are typically planned in work sets of four, with 100 total work minutes followed by a longer 15- to 20-minute break.

Here's what a Pomodoro cycle looks like:

1. Work for 25 minutes.

2. Take a 5-minute break.

3. Work for 25 more minutes.

4. Enjoy 5 minutes off.

5. Another 25 minutes of work.

6. Take a 5-minute break.

7. Work for a final 25 minutes.

8. Then enjoy a longer 15- to 20-minute break.

This technique is great for handling tasks that require long work sessions, ensuring that you don't hobble your productivity by spending too much time without a break. You can also use this cycle for your time blocking. But no matter the length of your work sessions, the important takeaway is to always schedule breaks.

Until your new working cycle becomes a habit, use a timer with an alarm to remind you when it's break time. Your phone or computer likely has a stopwatch or alarm function you can use; even a kitchen timer will do. Or search for a "Pomodoro" or "break timer" app.

Best Breaks Ever

There are so many quick ways to enjoy a refreshing break. No matter which you choose, be sure your break includes these two components: a change in your physical position and a shift of your attention to something different. For example, if you're working on your feet outside in the sun all day, take breaks in the shade or inside, sitting down. If you're spending hours sitting at your desk looking at your screen, get up, move your body, and don't look at any screens—phone included. Your breaks should give your eyes, body, and mind the rest they need to continue working.

Here are more ideas for your 5- to 10-minute breaks:

» Go for a walk outside, in the hallways, or up and down the stairs.

» Get something to eat or drink away from your work area.

» Look away from your screen at something 20 feet away.

» Take deep, slow breaths or meditate.

» Do some stretching, simple exercises, yoga, or tai chi poses.

» Get some fresh air and sunlight; sit on an outdoor bench or near a window.

» Have a quick chat with someone away from the work area, and don't discuss work.

DO A TIME AUDIT

Even after trying the strategies so far, you may still feel as if there's not enough time in your day. There's a lot of that going around, so don't worry. If these time-management techniques haven't helped you master your time as well as you'd like, you need to figure out why. How are you spending, and losing, your time?

What you need is a time audit. Just as it sounds, auditing your time simply means tracking your daily activities and creating a record of how long you spend on each. You'll identify any potential time-wasters and spot opportunities for improvement. This strategy works because most days, we're running on autopilot. We do things a certain way out of habit or routine. Think about it: When you get up in the morning, are you questioning what you need to do, or do you just do it? In the programmed lifestyles we lead, we're constantly zoned out and always losing track of time.

Tracking Your Time

Think of this as a time-management review, your chance to double-check that you're productively organizing your tasks and time. Just as you tracked your energy levels, use a notebook, journal, or document in your mobile device—something easy to keep with you—to track time spent on each of the day's events. No, you do not need to note every single thing you do; you can group and categorize similar tasks together. Keep the audit going for several days—the more data you can collect, the more accurate your audit will be. Then review the record and call out any timewasters (unproductive uses of time) and time sucks (spending more time on something than it deserves). Here's what tracking your time during a typical day of work could look like:

» **9:00 a.m. to 11:00 a.m.:** Checked emails and returned calls

» **11:00 a.m. to 12:00 p.m.:** Chatted with coworkers about vacation plans

- » **12:00 p.m. to 1:00 p.m.:** Lunch run to the mall

- » **1:00 p.m. to 4:00 p.m.:** Back-to-back meetings

- » **4:00 p.m. to 5:00 p.m.:** Back at desk, talking to coworkers on messenger

Let's review the results. From this simple audit above, we can see that time was wasted chatting with coworkers for two hours. Going to the mall looks like a time suck, since you could have packed a lunch.

Auditing your time not only creates a record, but it also makes you more aware of what you're doing throughout the day. It helps you snap out of autopilot mode. And it trains you to use your time consciously. The next time you start indulging in unproductive activities, you're more able to recognize it and resist.

If you find that you're still losing track of time and not making progress with the time-management strategies in this chapter, I encourage you to do a time audit. We make so many assumptions about the time we have each day and how we're spending it. The problem is, they're not always accurate. After completing your time audit, go back to the beginning and try these time-management strategies again. You will be more equipped to conquer procrastination when you're fully dialed-in, not leaving the day's schedule to chance or expecting to just figure it out along the way. Use these strategies and you'll be empowered to take an active role in ruling your time and conquering procrastination.

CHAPTER 4

Tap into Your Motivation

You've either got it or you don't.

There's something almost tangible about this invisible force called motivation. Without it, everything can feel like an uphill battle that you'd rather not be fighting; you feel sluggish, slow, or simply stuck in place. But with it, the wind is at your back, urging you forward; you feel confident, capable, and certain that procrastination doesn't stand a chance.

That's the power of motivation, which many of us rely on to get anything done. But motivation doesn't just appear out of nowhere. It has to be created. Waiting around to get motivated is like sitting in your car and waiting for it to start all on its own. Unless you turn the key and hit the gas, you're going nowhere. Motivation is your engine, and it's a powerful one, but it needs a spark to bring it to life. You must provide that spark. You can do that with your thoughts and with your actions, and you'll need to use both to conquer procrastination. In this chapter you'll learn how to rev up the engine of motivation whenever you need it most. Buckle up!

START WITH "WHY"

To connect with your motivation, to learn how to reach it whenever you need it, you have to understand where yours comes from. You have to find the source. And for this, you need to channel that curious child you once were, whose favorite question was "Why?" The source of your motivation is the answer to this very simple question. Whatever motivates you, the source is deeply personal, and only you can find it. Discovering your "why" requires one thing above all: complete honesty with yourself. You need to know your "why" and take ownership of it. That's the only way that this will work. Take a deep breath, and let's dive into finding your "why."

To start, consider any plans and dreams you have for your future. Think about all the priorities, tasks, and goals you've identified in the previous chapters. Review your notes, look at what you wrote, and ask yourself, *Why? What's it all for? What's the connection?* Find the greater purpose that unites them all. Your "why" might be a complete sentence or just a few words: *I want to help others. My health matters most. I need to have financial freedom for my family.* There are no rules, no right or wrong answers, as long as you're being open and honest with yourself.

Your "why" might come easily to you. Perhaps you've always been aware of it, sensed it hovering on the edge of your thinking as you made decisions in life. But these aren't the sort of questions we're used to asking ourselves, so it's completely normal to need time for deeper reflection to find an answer. After a certain age, we stop being the curious children who searched for meaning and an explanation for everything, and it can be difficult to find our way back to that mindset. If you have a hard time discovering your "why," here are some reflection questions to help:

- » Where does achieving your tasks lead you?

- » Why did you write those particular to-dos?

- » Why did you rank them the way you did?

» What life do you want for yourself?

» Why does accomplishing your goals matter?

» Why do you want to achieve this goal?

» How will it change your life?

Take as long as you need. As you search within yourself for answers, you might need to get up and go for a walk, journal for a bit, or even have a conversation with someone close to you. Please do whatever you need to do to process and then answer these questions. Answering them will help you see the purpose behind each action you take, every goal you set, and even the dreams you hold dear.

Let Me Count the "Whys"

You might be wondering if someone can have more than one "why." Yes, of course! No rules except honesty, remember? With the competing priorities and complex lives that most of us have, it's understandable that we would have more than one motivation. We struggle to balance our time, money, and energy between work and life or between passions and priorities. Perhaps you're a stay-at-home parent with your own business, a full-time student with a job, or someone with any combination of roles and responsibilities. For many of us, the seesaw tips back and forth daily. Life is complicated, and your "whys" can be, too.

If you are struggling to find your strongest reason, your one "why" for conquering procrastination, use the list below to help. Here are five distinct types of "whys" you might have; each is powerful in its unique way:

» PRACTICAL: It's all about survival, and what you need to do to secure your basic needs like water, food, sleep, and shelter.

» EGO: This is the "why" that strokes your pride and makes you feel important and special. It's your confidence, self-esteem, and sense of self-worth.

» COMMUNAL: It's not just about you—it's about others, too. This category includes your family, dependents, relationships, or the larger community.

» SOCIETAL: Your culture's prevailing social norms inform this reason, giving you a sense of what's wrong and right, good and bad.

» PUBLIC: Many of us have a version of "why" that we share with others when we're ashamed or insecure about our deeper reasons.

What's it all for? For your ego, for your family or survival? Do you have more than one answer? Which feels strongest right now? Whatever your deepest reason is, accept it and give yourself to it. Let it empower, strengthen, and motivate you to get things done.

USE VISUALIZATION

There's so much truth to the adage that seeing is believing. But what you might not know is that "seeing" starts in the mind. We're talking about visualization, and it's not nearly as mysterious or mystical as you might think. In fact, you use visualization every day without realizing it. Every single time you envision a worst-case scenario, let your imagination run wild, or picture yourself doing something, you are, in fact, using the power of visualization. And chances are you've been using this power to make your life difficult. How often do you let your mind conjure up images that feed your self-doubt, fears, worries, and other negative emotions? When you do, you play right into your procrastination triggers.

The more your mind visualizes an outcome, the more you see it in your mind, and the more you believe it. What if you could hack this ability, making it motivate you instead of discouraging you? Here's an example: You're assigned a task for the first time, and you start thinking it's going to be difficult. You picture yourself having to work harder than ever, staying up late to get it done. Before you lift a finger, you've already written the story, played it out in your mind, and believe it to the point that you can't even get started. But what if you used visualization to flip the script? What if you envisioned yourself excited about this new challenge, looking forward to the new task and ready to prove yourself? You see your hard work being recognized and how impressed everyone will be with your ideas. You visualize how your amazing work leads you to even greater opportunities.

You may have heard that visualization is a technique that's long been used by elite athletes as part of their training. Experts have found that by visualizing yourself accomplishing a task, essentially performing the actions in your mind, you improve your performance when you carry out these actions in the real world. Sometimes known as "mental practice" or "mental rehearsal," visualization has been proven again and again to help elite competitors perform at their highest level. And it will help you, too. Visualization sparks motivation in the mind before you even make a real-life move. See it in your mind, play it out, take action, and succeed. With visualization, you're engaged with your task before procrastination has a chance to get its foot in the door.

Easy Visualization Exercise

Ready to try it? This simple visualization exercise takes just a few minutes and is easy to add to your daily routine. When you're first using it, you might need a quiet space or need to step away to be alone. But as you practice, you'll be able call on this technique anywhere by just closing your eyes. Here are the five steps:

STEP 1: **Know what it's all for.** To visualize, you need a vision of your future. With your "why" firmly in mind, you already know what you want to achieve. You know where you're going and what this is all for. It's meaningful to you and very personal. Close your eyes and bring your goal to mind.

STEP 2: **Practice what needs to get done.** What do you need to do today to achieve success? What tasks and to-dos need to get done? Clear your mind and see yourself getting started, going through the movements of each task, and succeeding each time. Call up the details in your imagination and go through each step, every motion of the task, like a golfer imagining a flawless swing or an artist envisioning the perfect painting.

STEP 3: **See yourself as successful.** What does success look like to you? What does your end result and destination look like? Set the scene in your mind and play it out. Where are you? Who's with you? Who's congratulating you? How perfect is the final product? What pleasure are you getting as you close the file or cross the finish line? Fill in all the details and see everything in vivid color.

STEP 4: **Know what it feels like.** How does it feel to make it happen? What emotions does this moment of success spark in you? Are you happy, excited, proud, relieved? Feel all the feels and name the emotions.

STEP 5: **Now, take action.** Visualization only works when followed up by action. Take these positive emotions with you, carry them throughout the day, and let them motivate you as you get things done. When your motivation begins to fade, continue to picture yourself accomplishing your tasks for the day and then make it happen.

Visualization is a simple mental training exercise that helps you see yourself succeeding. It's the feeling of what your accomplishments will be like, experienced in the now. Doing this helps you conquer procrastination by creating an emotional connection to your future self. If you see how amazing life could be once you've accomplished your tasks, you're less likely to put them off.

CREATE A VISION BOARD

What would your goals, hopes, dreams, and aspirations for the future look like if you could take them out of your head and hang them on a wall? A vision board is how you figure that out. It's a real-world depiction of the same success you see and feel in your visualization exercises, composed of images you collect and curate. Each image on your vision board helps you relate to the ideal life you're working toward; specific scenes, environments, objects, scenarios, words, and even abstract imagery can evoke an emotion or idea. Once completed, your vision board provides an external motivator that you can focus on, meditate on, and be inspired by.

There are two main types: a physical vision board made from cut-out images fixed on a backing of some kind, or a digital one created using a collage-making application. Physical boards can be mounted in your home or office, and you can access them just by paying attention, inspiring you every time you walk by. But they take more time to make, as you need to collect your materials. Digital vision boards don't require as much time to put together (if you're handy with some basic image software) and they can be displayed easily on your devices—though you'll need a device to access them. Each format has its own strengths, and one isn't better than the other; it's a choice based on which works best for you.

Build Your Board

Ready to create your vision board? First, decide whether you'll make a physical or digital board, then follow the five steps below.

STEP 1: **Know what you want.** Your very first step is to be clear about what you want. Does that sound familiar? Thankfully, throughout this chapter you've already figured out your "why" and spent time visualizing what success looks like. So, what does your future life look like? Now's the time to write it down on paper. Use words, themes, and emotions to describe what you really want. Think about your personal and professional life. Remember the goals and priorities that you've also set for yourself, and feel free to go back to the previous chapters and notes you have taken and used. For example, your ideal life could be living in a happy home of your own. So, you could write down family, love, safe, cozy, or secure.

STEP 2: **Collect your materials.** You need some material to create your vision board. If you're making a physical board, you have several choices for the board itself: cardboard or Bristol board, cork, or even a magnet board. You'll need a way to attach images, so equip yourself with tape, pushpins, magnets, or whatever's appropriate. For a digital board, set yourself up with a graphics program of your choice, or search for a collage-creating app. With your board ready to go, you can start collecting images to add to it. Magazines are a good source; ask friends and family to contribute. Check yard sales and flea markets for illustrated books, newspapers, flyers, and other source material. For a digital board, create a file or directory where you can save favorite downloaded images.

STEP 3: **Choose your images.** Once you've amassed a substantial image collection, it's time to select the ones that represent your vision. Find a comfy and inspiring spot to slowly go through your magazines or other materials, or settle in with your laptop or phone. Have your word list on hand from step 1 and choose any images that convey or represent your desired life or the emotions you want to feel. Images might be a literal one (a house in the style you love) or just evoke a feeling (a shade of blue that reminds you of your childhood bedroom). You can also add words and phrases to your board, taking them from the source material or writing them out yourself: power, success, travel, happiness, joy—whatever fits your vision.

STEP 4: **Assemble.** With all your supplies and images collected, set aside an hour or two to put your vision board together. Arrange images and words on your board, moving them around until you're happy with the position they're in. When you look at your vision board, you should feel inspired and encouraged. That's when you know everything is in the right position. Once you're ready, you can affix everything to the board. If you're creating a digital board, complete the same steps, then save and print, if possible.

STEP 5: **Post.** The most important step for creating a vision board happens after you've completed it. Remember, your board is a visual representation of your future life. For it to help you as a visualization tool, you need to be able to see it daily. You can't tap into your motivation if you can't see it, can you? Hang your physical vision board on a wall or post it in a spot that you spend a lot of time in, such as your bedroom or office. Post your digital board as your desktop, phone, or tablet background, where you can see it daily. You want your board to live in a high-sight area so you can easily incorporate it into your daily visualization exercises, using the board as a tool to focus your mind on your future success.

REFRAME YOUR INNER MONOLOGUE

What's that? Did you say something? Nope, sorry, that's just you "talking" to yourself. You know what I mean—the way you can "hear" your voice inside your head, without actually hearing it. This is your inner monologue, and it encompasses everything from passing thoughts to replayed conversations and the full-on debates you have with yourself. Your consciousness streams endlessly, like a radio station only you can hear. When you're tuned in to it, that inner voice can be as loud as a rock concert. But even when you're not paying attention, it continues to play like background music in an elevator.

With all that inner chatter going on, what are you really saying to yourself? Do you even know? We can have up to 80,000 thoughts a day racing through our minds, so it's unsurprising that the quality of those thoughts can impact our mood and motivation. Your inner monologue can inspire and motivate, or discourage and depress. Sadly, it's estimated that, on average, 80 percent of a person's daily thoughts are negative. As these negative thought patterns continue, they can impact your emotions and potentially lead to conditions like depression and anxiety. And as you now know, negative emotions can trigger procrastination.

Like any bad habit, negative thinking can be replaced with a more productive, positive inner voice. People who have more positive thoughts are generally more optimistic, happier, and have healthier lives than those with more negative thoughts. When you're at your best, most positive, mentally, you feel more confident and capable of getting things done. So, our goal is to stop being held back by negative thoughts like *I can't do this,* or *This is just too hard,* and to cultivate more positive ones, such as, *I can get this done now* or *I'm up for the challenge.* By reframing your inner monologue with supportive self-talk, you're able to tap into your motivation. And not only does this work for your thoughts about things you need to accomplish, but it also works for your thoughts about yourself and your life.

Kick Negative Thoughts Out of Your Head

Your first step toward reframing your inner monologue is learning to identify negative thoughts so that you can replace them. These thoughts can range from self-doubt, jealousy, and self-limiting beliefs all the way to perfectionist thinking and indecisiveness. Sound familiar? Oh, hello there, procrastination-feeding thoughts—we meet again. By cutting off these negative thoughts at their source, you'll be able to conquer these procrastination triggers.

Let's give it a try. The two-step formula is to first identify a negative thought pattern and then respond with a more positive one. You need to remix that downer of a thought; that's how you start a positive dialogue with yourself and reframe your inner monologue. You have the power; you are in control. It's your brain, after all. Here are three common types of negative thinking, and examples of how you can reframe them:

SELF-CRITICISM AND JUDGEMENT: Have you ever thought, *I suck, I'm an idiot,* or *I'm such a loser?* What other not-so-nice names do you have for yourself? Maybe someone said this to you once, and their criticism just keeps echoing in your mind, to the point where you even believe it yourself. Ever done something that made you feel awkward and foolish? Can't stop thinking about that either, right? Change the narrative when these thoughts arise by speaking to yourself in a loving, compassionate, and caring way. Anytime a self-critical, judgmental thought pops up, find the opposite of the negative word and use it to describe yourself. You can respond to yourself with *I'm amazing, I'm so smart,* or *I'm the best.* Say that positive statement over and over to yourself, drowning out the negative with every repetition.

JEALOUSY AND COMPARISON: In our social media–heavy world it's way too easy to compare yourself to other people and to be jealous of their success. Thoughts like, *Why bother? She's better; I'll never be as good as he is*; or *Their lives are so easy, they have everything* can just dry up your motivation. These thoughts make you feel less-than, self-conscious, and they lead you to doubt your abilities. Turn the thought upside down: Instead of being jealous, be inspired by their success, like this: *Wow, if she can do it, so can I.* Focus on what makes you uniquely capable. There's only one you—remember that. Always choose compassion toward yourself over comparison with someone else.

LIMITING BELIEFS AND SELF-DOUBTS: We all hold certain beliefs to be true, beliefs that limit what's possible for us. Common examples are, *I can't do this. I'll never make it*, or even convictions about our circumstances, like *I don't have enough time/money/energy.* What limiting beliefs are plaguing your mind? Pull them out at the roots by challenging them with evidence to the contrary. Reply with an, *Actually, I can [insert accomplishment here].* Remember your proudest moments—times when you did something challenging, or experienced success—and meditate on those to counteract self-doubt.

MAKE IT A GAME

Whether it's racing your workout buddy to the finish line or trying to land your crumpled-up piece of paper in the wastebasket from across the room, everyone loves trying to win. This motivational trick is used everywhere, from educational games for children to shopper loyalty programs that encourage you to spend more. The best challenges make commitment and consistency feel like a game, swapping out undesirable emotions for playful and enjoyable ones. And the most successful motivating games offer a reward for participating and a prize for winning. Instead of feeling stressed or anxious, you feel excited and energized—which makes this a perfect strategy to hack your motivation.

So, I challenge you to make a game of it. Are you in? Let's transform your list of today's must-dos into an exciting challenge that gets you moving. For this to be successful, your game needs two key elements: the rules of the game, and a prize for completing it. Keep the rules simple and outline what your challenge is, including the element of time for added excitement. You've probably watched game shows before, so you know that the ticking timer is really what gets people going. If you're one of those people who needs the pressure of a deadline to get things done (remember the thrill-seeker from chapter 1?) this is how you satisfy that need without having to procrastinate.

Ready, Set, Motivate

The specific rules for each challenge will depend entirely on what needs to get done, but here are a few examples to get you going:

» **Got an overflowing inbox at work?** Set the timer and see how many emails you can reply to in 20 minutes. Note your score and try to beat it next time.

» **At the gym and losing steam?** Push yourself to do just two more miles, laps, or reps. Or set a timer and see how many repetitions of your workout you can complete in 10 minutes.

» **Have a paper due tomorrow?** Grab your stopwatch and see how long it takes you to write 500 words, or how many words you can write in 30 minutes.

» **Is the house a complete mess?** Give yourself 15 uninterrupted minutes to speed clean one room or vacuum all the floors.

You can add another element of gamification by bringing in other challengers. Invite a friend, colleague, or family member to play your game, too. Get your kids to participate in your clean-up game or a workout buddy to go the extra mile with you. This way, you both can tap into another person's motivations, too.

This strategy works even better when you have a reward for completing your challenge. Keep things simple by permitting yourself to enjoy a small treat. Perfect prizes include allowing yourself to relax on the sofa reading a magazine, having a sweet snack, or even watching a video online.

How about we turn up the heat a little? If you're looking for ways to keep the motivation flowing, schedule daily challenges for yourself. Use a calendar or habit tracker app to record your progress every day. Add a big check mark each time you complete a challenge, or do 10 in a row to earn something extra special. With each day, you're making a habit of this new motivating ritual, as well as building momentum. This is a critical step in leveling up, because habit kicks in when motivation fades, keeping you going no matter how you feel. Plus, the daily repetition enables you to develop habits that become second nature. The next time you pick up your list of must-dos and find yourself not-so-motivated, you'll instinctively make a game of it.

USE A TAKE-ACTION RITUAL

Let's be honest—we've all had times when we were ready to take action but still struggled to find the motivation. Times when knowing exactly what we want and need to do should be enough to get us going, but isn't. Now and then you need something extra. And that's okay. Because you're about to learn how to shift yourself into action, no matter how immobile you feel.

What you need is to create a "take-action ritual." It's a simple sequence of activities that takes 10 minutes or less to complete, and prepares your mind and body for action. Your take-action ritual is built of acts that help you feel focused, confident, ready, and willing to get to work. The details are completely up to you. You can do anything and everything that gets you motivated, including some of the strategies you've learned in this chapter, like using your vision board or reframing your inner monologue. I'll take you through my own ritual to give you some ideas.

Sample Take-Action Ritual

You can do this anywhere you need to. All you need for it to work is a willingness to get motivated.

1. Take a few deep breaths—inhale and exhale slowly. Relax your shoulders, release all the tension, let the stress fall away with every exhale.

2. Think about your "why," what matters most for you today and what you need to get done. If you have a vision board, you can use it as a visualization tool here.

3. Ask yourself, *What tiny, intentional action can I take right now? What baby step toward success can I achieve?* Visualize yourself doing it.

4. Write it down on a piece of paper. This is your number one must-do for today.

Now add steps here that make you feel calm, focused, and ready, like:

5. Make a cup of tea, get a hydrating drink, or grab a quick snack.

6. Get comfortable in your workspace and create a distraction-free environment. Close the door, ask not to be disturbed, put your phone out of sight, or use noise-canceling headphones.

7. Breathe in, breathe out, and just get started. Don't even think about it. As you start, speak encouragingly to yourself. Remind yourself that you can do this, that you're ready and you're going to get so much done today.

Anytime I find myself slipping into procrastination, those simple steps snap me into action. They wake up my motivation and reignite my commitment. As I go through my ritual, my subconscious mind knows that it's time to work, time to get in the game. Think of this as tricking yourself into focusing.

Try it yourself, changing up the steps until you land on the ritual that does the trick. The best rituals fit seamlessly into your daily routine so you can use them every day to stay motivated. Stick to your ritual and eventually you'll make a habit of taking action after you complete it. Each time you begin your ritual, you're signaling to yourself that it's time to focus, get to work, and get things done. No more excuses. You're the director of your life, you are the one in control, so you can even say "action" out loud—it might sound silly, but this really does work. If you can make a habit of getting motivated, you'll be unstoppable, and procrastination won't stand a chance.

CHAPTER 5

Get Focused, Stay Focused

On a scale of one to five, how focused are you? Can you stay concentrated on certain tasks for a significant chunk of time? Or do you find your mind wandering and distractions interrupting you?

Staying focused on your tasks and goals doesn't happen by accident; it's achieved through practice. If you're someone who struggles with concentration, don't worry. As you learn and test-drive the focusing techniques in this chapter, you'll become a master of focus. And even if the first five minutes of a challenging project feels like forever, you'll be able to stay dialed in until you're done. Now that you have motivation and time management working to get you started on your tasks, it's time to develop the focus that carries you through to the finish. Let's get focused.

Do you remember when you were little, and you'd get caught watching TV when you should have been doing your homework? Yeah, you still need that kind of reminder from time to time to get things done. Ever had the experience of being on a roll, feeling completely engaged in what you're working on, only to have someone interrupt you, bringing your momentum to a crashing halt? Yup, that's the other side of this coin. Both examples demonstrate why you need to let the people in your life know what's going on: They can keep you on track when you're drifting (accountability), and give you time and space to focus (support). It's all about communication with the folks around you. Without it, you're missing out on the positive reinforcement and encouragement of those who care about you. A lack of communication leaves you vulnerable to being constantly interrupted, distracted, and sent off-course.

Support and Accountability

Be honest right now: Do you feel supported in your goals? Or do you feel as if you're doing it all on your own? The latter is a very relatable situation that so many of us face. For whatever reason—a fear of rejection or judgement, perhaps, or the lack of a support system— you may find yourself going it alone. But what if you didn't have to? Imagine how different things could be if you had a friend, family member, or coworker in your corner, giving you support and encouraging you when you needed it most, even working with you every step of the way. I know it's scary to let people in, but the potential reward outweighs any possible risk.

Here are a few examples of how others can support you in reaching your goals:

» You've started a new diet that you're nervous about. By sharing this with your lunchmates, you're enabling them to support you by keeping you on track, but also by not tempting you. They'll be more mindful of eating junk food in front of you, or offering you food you can't eat.

» Exams are in a few weeks, and you're feeling stressed. By connecting with a classmate and forming a study group, you make it easier to focus. Together you can have study dates, keep each other on track, and share notes. By emphasizing to your friends that you need to focus on exams, you signal that they shouldn't invite you out on a Tuesday night.

For this to work, you need to share your plans and open up about your goals with people you trust. There's no need to shout everything from the rooftops, but informing someone who knows and possibly shares your priorities is invaluable for staying focused. There are going to be moments when you're feeling unmotivated, and you'll need someone to lift you up, someone on the sidelines who will cheer you on and get you back on your feet and in the game. Don't deprive yourself of these lifelines.

Boundaries and Balance

Good fences make good neighbors; likewise, clear boundaries make good balance. Without a clear distinction between when you need uninterrupted time to work and when you're available to others, you are inviting interruptions and distractions into your daily life. Those boundaries are for you to follow, too, so you don't throw your life out of balance by mixing work tasks with home life.

Here's how boundaries can work for you:

» You're a stay-at-home parent who only gets 30 minutes a day to yourself. This time is to focus on you and the things you need to do. If you don't communicate this "me time" as sacred and important with your partner and children, they'll interrupt you for sure.

» You're a busy full-time employee whose workday ends at 5:00 p.m. You make sure your colleagues know that you're not going to be replying to emails all night. If they need you, they have to contact you before 5:00 p.m. or wait until the next day.

Setting boundaries can be uncomfortable at first, but it's for your benefit. It all starts with holding yourself accountable to this idea of balance—keeping your personal life safe and the rest of your commitments, like school and work, in their respective time slots and then sharing that information with those who need to know. Doing so will not only help you stay focused but also save you from burnout and from neglecting the other parts of your life.

TALK YOURSELF INTO IT

Have you ever tried to talk someone into doing something they didn't want to do? It's not so easy, is it? "You've got this" and "Get it done" only get you so far. Especially when you're talking to yourself. In those moments where you're just not feeling it, you're distracted, or you're thinking about giving up, you'll need all your powers of persuasion to snap yourself into getting the task completed.

So, how do you unlock your powers of self-persuasion? How do you talk yourself into staying focused? Persuasion works when your argument is accompanied by a real, rational, or emotional appeal. In your most stubborn and sluggish moments, when you've dug your heels into inaction, you have to know what motivational buttons to push. You cannot be afraid to go there with yourself. Your reasons and your rationalization for taking action have to be personal to you. Fortunately, you happen to be an expert when it comes to your own motivation. It's all about combining positive self-talk with the right emotional and rational arguments.

Top 10 Ways to Talk to Yourself

Let's go over some self-talk ground rules. Rule number one: Always be compassionate and caring toward yourself. That means you're not judging past or present procrastination, inaction, or any other reasons why you're losing focus. Let all those reasons go so you can move forward. Rule number two: Be supportive and encouraging with yourself. Life's hard enough; there's no need to bring yourself down. Keep it positive, okay?

Here are 10 ways to talk yourself out of a funk and into action:

1. **USE YOUR "WHYS":** What's the purpose of this action? Remind yourself of your deepest motivation, your "whys." For example, "I need to get this done because I'm committed to graduating on time."

2. **REITERATE THE IMPORTANCE:** Why is this task so significant? What future action depends on you completing it? Bring these facts front-of-mind. For example, "If I don't file my taxes, I won't qualify for the tax rebate."

3. **THINK URGENCY:** Is there a deadline or due date? Why does this need to get done now? Tell yourself why it's timely. For instance, "I need to do this now—this application is due at midnight tonight."

4. **MAKE IT EASIER:** How can you simplify this task? Break down complex tasks into easier ones. Set a time block and plan breaks. Something like, "This is easy! All I have to do today is read a chapter, then I can go hang out in the park."

5. **REMEMBER PAST SUCCESSES:** Have you done something similar in the past? What's your biggest accomplishment? Remind yourself of how capable you are. For instance, "This is nothing. Last year, I wrote a 10,000-word paper on no sleep. I can do this."

6. **TALK ABOUT YOUR GOALS:** What's your goal again? Tell yourself about your goal and why this task aligns with it. An example might be, "I need to prep and cook healthier meals so I can lose 10 pounds this spring."

7. **SEE YOUR VISION:** What is your vision of the future? What does success look and feel like? Use visualization to remind yourself. Study your vision board. A visualization might look like, "Filling out this application to start a charity is my first step toward collecting donations that will change lives."

8. **DO THE HARD THING FIRST:** Remind yourself how good it will feel when this challenging task is out of the way, how stress-free the rest of your day will be when you get it done. For instance, "If I take 20 minutes to clean the kitchen, I'll have the entire day to relax."

9. **TAKE BABY STEPS:** What can you accomplish in 10 minutes or less? Is there a small task, a first step, that you can start? "It will only take 10 minutes to send this important email to my lawyer."

10. **ASK A FRIEND:** What's the most encouraging thing a friend has ever said to you? What were those inspiring words of wisdom? Say them to yourself right now. Or tell yourself what you might say to a friend who was in your position. "It doesn't have to be perfect; it just needs to get done."

There you have the 10 ways to talk yourself into taking action. The next time you start losing focus, use your powers of persuasion to talk yourself into it. You are now certified to use these Jedi mind tricks on yourself.

MEET YOUR MANTRA

When your mind starts to wander, when you feel your focus slipping, the solution could be as simple as a repeated word or phrase, also known as a "mantra." For thousands of years, mantras have been used in meditative practices to calm and focus the mind. Mantras allow you to clear away distracting thoughts, worries of the day, and everything that's interfering with your focus, redirecting your wandering attention and internal monologue to the here and now. Whether you say them out loud or in your head, these redirecting mantras help you achieve greater focus the more you use them.

Even though using mantras is an ancient technique, modern science is only now discovering its true potential. The limited scientific studies that have been done confirm that repeated speech affects the area of the brain known as the "default mode network." This network of brain cells is most active when you're daydreaming, self-reflecting, or thinking about the past or the future. Brain imaging confirms that using mantras quiets brain activity in this area. Repeating silent mantras to yourself enables you to turn down the volume on your internal monologue so you can focus on the present.

So, how do you choose a mantra? Does it matter what you say? The most time-honored mantra is the single syllable "Om," traditionally used in yoga, breathing, and meditation practices. You can practice using this vibrational sound by slowly repeating "Ahh," then "Ohh," ending with an "Mm." Om is just one of many refocusing mantras to choose from. Don't worry if this is outside your comfort zone. Almost any other word, phrase, or sentence will do. In fact, let's choose one that's just for you.

How to Find Your Mantra

What makes your mantra work is the silent repetition. It doesn't matter how many words it is, as long as they encourage you to refocus your mind. You can choose a word, a phrase, or even a full sentence and commit it to memory—it's just a matter of what works for you. Choose something that captures your attention and helps center your mind. The best mantras will speak directly to your situation, meaning, if you're feeling anxious and worried, it should calm you. Here's some guidance:

Choose a word. What word speaks to you right now or moves you? It can be a word that relates to what you need (such as "focus" or "action"), to your goals and priorities (such as "family" or "health"), or an aspiration that captures your attention (like "motivated" or "directed").

Pick a phrase. What do you need to hear when times are tough? Is there a phrase that has some special meaning for you? Think of a few words about yourself: *I am enough, I am successful*; phrases about how you want to feel, such as *I am calm, I am confident* or motivating sayings like *My thoughts become reality*, or *Today is the best day ever*.

Use a quote. Do you have a favorite quotation? A saying that really resonates with you? Memorize and repeat it to yourself. (For example, *Done is better than perfect. Nothing is impossible*.)

Sing a song. A phrase from a song that's meaningful to you can be your mantra, too. You already know the lyrics; sing it to yourself. Songs like "Stronger" by Kelly Clarkson, "Beautiful Day" by U2, "Survivor" by Destiny's Child and "Girl on Fire" by Alicia Keys to name just a few anthems-turned-mantras.

I've shared some of my favorite mantras with you in the above examples. Mantras have gotten me through more situations than I have space to share. They have fought and won against self-doubt, fears, worry, and every thought in between.

SINGLETASKING, PART TWO

Focusing isn't just about zeroing in on the task at hand. It's equally important to be able to ignore everything else. You cannot focus on what's most important and urgent if you're also thinking about what's next. Being truly focused requires you to be mindful of the current moment and single-minded in your attention. And that isn't easy.

That's why almost everyone multitasks, even though they really shouldn't. Multitasking is not only bad for your productivity (as we discussed in chapter 3), but it's also equally destructive to your focus. Remember, you can only truly focus on one thing at a time. You're, by definition, unfocused if you're trying to do multiple tasks at once. Just accept it: Despite what you've been led to believe, you cannot successfully stay focused on multiple tasks at the same time. Instead, you're effectively splitting your attention—and your brain capacity along with it. Think about a time when you tried to talk to someone on the phone and another person in the room with you at the same time. Or attempted to drive and text simultaneously (I know you've done it). It doesn't work.

Multitasking and Task-Switching

The science agrees that multitasking is problematic at best. Here's why: Your brain has limited working memory capacity. When you try to do too much at once, you slow down your reactions and limit your responses. And that's not all. If you're multitasking while using technology, your brain cannot decide which of the two tasks is more important. For example, if you're on social media and doing your homework, your brain doesn't recognize that your homework is more important. This is true for almost everyone on the planet, with only 2 percent of humanity able to successfully multitask. (I'd bet they're the same people who also never procrastinate—if they really exist at all. I've certainly never met anyone like that.)

For the other 98 percent of us, the case against multitasking doesn't end there. An added complication to multitasking is the cost of switching tasks. When you multitask, what's really going on is that you're frequently switching your attention between two or more tasks. For example, suppose you work for five minutes, pick up your phone for two, go back to work for three more, then answer an email for five. If we add all this time up, you wouldn't have spent all 15 minutes on three tasks. You woud be wasting several minutes to "task lag," the time lost as your brain slows down to switch tasks. The more complex the tasks you're shifting to and from, the more time is lost. It's even worse when a task is unfamiliar to you. To put this into a quantifiable number that will scare you into quitting multitasking forever: One study estimated that you lose 40 percent of your weekly productivity to task-switching—that is nothing but a major time suck.

The way forward is clear: You need to singletask. Multitasking is not only an ineffective habit that leads to loss of focus but also costs you time in the end. Instead of letting your attention drift when you're working on one thing and suddenly remembering something else that needs doing, write that second task down and tell yourself you'll get to it later. Another great strategy is to schedule a day and time for dealing with unfinished tasks. I always ensure that I have a catch-up day to get to loose ends, keeping my mind free to focus on what I'm doing right now. And remember to use time blocking (page 46) so you have time set aside for each task.

REMOVE DISTRACTIONS

Did you know that it can take up to 30 minutes to refocus on a task after being distracted? And in this hyperconnected world we live and work in, distractions of all sorts are constantly vying for your attention. Each pop-up notification on your screen or spam caller on your phone (we check our phones every 12 minutes, on average), each time your kids need you to moderate a dispute, or a coworker pops by to chat, you can go from being in the zone to being zoned out in no time flat.

The Best Distraction Beaters

Ready to beat back the distractions that are draining your focus? Here are the best ways to limit distractions while focusing on tasks at home, work, school, or on the computer.

DISTRACTIONS AT HOME:

» **Mark your territory.** Go into another room of the house. Close or even lock the door if possible. As mentioned, you need to communicate with those around you so they know to leave you alone. But it also helps to stay off everyone's radar and to add a visual cue so no one forgets. Like a sign on your door that reads "Do not disturb."

» **When you're working, just work.** Don't blend work time with household chores, cleaning, cooking, and errands. Reserve those for your lunch hours or breaks.

» **Silence your phone.** Especially if you constantly receive spam calls or frequent interrupting notifications.

» **Have childcare in place.** Despite everyone's best intentions, kids inevitably demand your attention if you're home. Arrange for someone to keep your child occupied—and enforce boundaries—so you can concentrate on your work.

DISTRACTIONS AT WORK:

» **Shush.** Silence instant messaging services and other alerts; turn off pop-up notifications. Instead of reacting to messages as they come in, reply to them all at a set time.

» **Stick to your scheduled breaks.** Set a 5-minute alarm on your phone or computer when walking around the office. It's easy to get pulled into conversations with coworkers on the way to the printer or washroom. But the alert will remind you that you've got to get back to it.

» **Rethink meetings.** Workplaces have meetings for almost everything, so be certain that you need to attend before going. Check with the organizer about the agenda, objectives, and goals, and consider if those goals align with your own. Only go to essential meetings.

DISTRACTIONS AT SCHOOL:

» **Hide your phone.** Leave your phone on silent and out of sight in class or while studying. Make it a little difficult to check your phone; keep it buried in a bag or backpack so you'll think twice about using it to look up every little thing. Instead, write questions down and search for the answers online at the right time.

» **Sit up front during lectures.** With fewer people in front of you, you're less likely to get distracted by others and what they're doing.

» **Use silent study rooms.** When looking for a place to study, always choose a silent room or a quiet area in the library. Or book a silent study room with like-minded classmates.

COMPUTER DISTRACTIONS:

» **Turn off notifications.** Most computers, phones, and devices have push notifications set up by default that pop up and ping for all sorts of (usually trivial) reasons. Go into your settings and turn them off. Check for updates at designated times.

» **Close your email.** Leave your email inbox closed throughout the day; the extra steps needed to access it will dissuade you from constantly checking to see when emails come in. Have a designated time each day for checking email. If you don't need to reply on a daily basis, designate one day a week to clear your inbox. Set up an automatic response message to manage people's expectations about replies.

» **Limit browser distractions.** If you're constantly tempted to click on ads or news headlines in your browser, turn off these features and use an ad blocker.

CREATE THE RIGHT ENVIRONMENT

Removing interruptions and disruptions is just one part of a larger strategy to create the right working environment. You don't have to be an interior designer or feng shui expert to recognize that every space and place has its own vibe and energy. Some are soothing;

others are chaotic, and our understanding of these feelings is usually based on emotional connections and past experiences. You're more relaxed, calm, and mentally creative when your physical surroundings are aligned with your purpose.

Whatever environment you're in, sometimes it's just a change of scenery that you need—which is another reason to make sure that you schedule regular breaks during your work time. If your inspiration is dried up and you're distracted, stepping away to a new environment for a short break can give you a sweet hit of dopamine, a feel-good brain chemical that relaxes you. Get it pumping through your brain and body by going for a walk, doing some light exercise, dancing to a song you love, or even taking a shower.

Space Exploration

Let's find the right space for you to be your most productive self. Here's a list of commonly used locations that foster focus, creativity, and inspiration. Odds are you can find one near you.

» **CAFÉ OR COFFEE SHOP:** From the aroma of brewing coffee to the hum of chatter, coffee shops are perfect places for productivity. You can usually find free Wi-Fi, comfortable seating, and affordable drinks and eats.

» **COWORKING SPACE:** Need an office space without the office expenses? Check out a coworking space in your community. That's a shared working space where you can rent a single desk, cubical, or room. Some cities even have free coworking spaces in community centers and business complexes. Search online for "coworking space near me."

» **LIBRARY OR BOOKSTORE:** With free admission and no food-buying required, libraries and bookstores provide scholarly inspiration and a calm vibe. They typically also have private rooms you can reserve.

» **OUT AND ABOUT:** Inspirational spots are all around you— explore and you're bound to find one. From your building's lobby with all those comfy chairs to the park at the end of the road, stretch your legs and find the right working spot for you. Community centers, hotel lobbies, museums, and even sitting areas in malls may have spots where you can work comfortably.

And don't forget to evaluate the space you're already working in. Is it too dark or too bright? Too cold or too hot? Perhaps it's messy and disorganized? Is it too loud, or possibly too quiet? Simple adjustments can have a bigger impact than you might expect. Please be responsible; this is not an invitation to start a big, expensive home-office renovation. But what about a comfier chair, a cabinet to hide the clutter, or some colorful art or potted plants?

JUST START SAYING NO

For whatever reason, whether it is avoiding conflict, a desire to please people, or fear of disappointing others, saying no can be a struggle. It's not generosity and willingness to be helpful that's the problem here. It's that saying yes to every request leads to you overextending yourself, limiting your ability to focus on what matters to you. When you're saying yes to everything and everyone, you're essentially saying no to yourself. Every yes comes with a commitment of time, energy, and in some cases, money or other resources. By saying yes, you're surrendering assets that should be going toward your own goals, priorities, and pursuits.

Of course, sometimes yes is the right answer. Before you say it, always pause and consider if you really should. If you're uncomfortable saying no, try these strategies.

Practice drawing boundaries with smaller, less significant commitments. When someone asks for a favor that someone else could easily handle—to proofread an email, maybe, or help bring some boxes to the recycling bins—apologize and say it's not a good time. Soon you'll realize that the world won't end, and people won't hate you just because you turn down a request.

Give yourself some time. If you can't muster up a no in the moment, say that you'll have to think about it and check your schedule. Follow up with a gentle decline after you've looked at your schedule and must-do list.

Just be honest. Being truthful with yourself and others is the best policy. Don't be afraid to say you can't do it, even if it's something you've always done or have been doing for a while. Odds are, the person you're talking to is also overbooked and will totally understand.

Your No-Do List

Before you say yes, ensure that any potential commitment passes this test. Make saying no your default response to the things on this list:

» **Things that aren't important to you, or urgent.** You know, category 4 on your master list (page 32). Remember prioritization 101: if it's not essential or time-sensitive, you need to say no.

» **Things you don't care about.** Listen, you can't be invested emotionally in every single thing. If this isn't something you're supportive of, then don't agree to it.

» **Anything you're guilted into or are doing out of obligation.** Never do something simply because you feel others will judge you if you don't.

» **Everything contrary to your goals and priorities.** You know where your priorities lie—now align your actions with them. If something pulls you away from your intended goal, say no.

» **Things that don't serve your "why" or that you're doing for the wrong reasons.** Are you doing something for social status or to show others up? Consider the possibility that your intentions are misaligned.

You also need to pay attention to when you need to say no to yourself. Seeing something through to completion is the highest achievement of focus; ignore those shiny ideas that pop up like notifications in your mind. Have you ever started toward a goal but given up midway to begin something else? Is your home filled with projects you've started, stopped, and moved on from? We'd all like to think that every idea we have is brilliant, but the best practice is to objectively stay focused on the task at hand. It's better to complete one task than to have 10 tasks that are 10 percent completed. Instead of reacting and chasing these ideas right away, write them down, think them through, and plan to get back to them at the opportune time (whenever that may be). Saying no to yourself doesn't mean you can never do whatever you're considering; it just means you know there's a right time—and it's not now.

CHAPTER 6

Give Yourself Incentives

Do you love sign-up bonuses and free gifts with purchase? How about an extra month of membership if you join now or a buy-one-get-one deal? We all enjoy getting a little something extra for our efforts. The same can be said for our commitment to conquering procrastination. Sure, gaining the confidence and know-how to get things done on time is its own priceless reward. But what if I told you that you can also get some tasty icing on that cake? This is your incentive to read this chapter.

Incentives are motivational rewards you receive for completing an action. They encourage you to get things done and meet your objectives. The best part is, you're the one who gets to decide how you'll celebrate your good behavior. The choices are many: Incentives come in all shapes and sizes, from instant gratifications and small luxuries to big indulgences. So, let's top off everything you've learned by exploring how to motivate and encourage yourself with rewards for all your hard work.

INSTANT GRATIFICATION

Why does it feel so good to cross something off your to-do list? That's gratification—the warm sentiment that's a perfect mix of pride, joy, and happiness. It makes you smile, laugh, and even do that funny, happy dance you do when no one's watching. It's an emotion that encourages and motivates you to be even more productive. And you can use gratification, instant or not, to refuel your daily motivation and give yourself the extra spring in your step you need to take on your next task.

The most common type of gratification we're all familiar with is the instant variety. In fact, with modern technology, we live in a world driven by the desire for immediate recognition and gratification. We want it now, we want it faster, and we don't want to wait for anything. You might be able to microwave your dinner, email a message across the continent, or watch anything you want with a few clicks, but you can't always get everything done with the same expediency. Your tasks, goals, and even your dreams take patience, time, commitment, and consistency. You can't snap your fingers and make your to-do list disappear (if only!). At first glance it seems that the concept of instant gratification is in direct conflict with conquering procrastination. Or is it?

Make Instant Gratification Work for You

Remember how we learned in chapter 1 that we turn to procrastination because it gives us the instant gratification of avoiding a troubling emotion? Well, that was the *old* you. You've come a long way, so it's time to turn instant gratification from an impediment into an incentive. Instead of getting your instant gratification from checking social media when you should be working, you'll gain this warm, fuzzy feeling from getting something done.

Practice this move in small doses first with lesser, not-so-time-intensive tasks done as quickly as you can. What can you get done in 15 minutes or less? Here are a few examples:

» **Your house is a mess, and your in-laws are visiting this weekend.** To feel positive instant gratification, get started in one room or on one task you can complete in 15 minutes, like doing the dishes or tidying up your bedroom. Then stop and admire all you've accomplished.

» **You have hundreds of unopened junk emails in your inbox.** Unsubscribe from 10 newsletters, then delete as many junk emails as you can in 20 minutes. Then, go to your trash folder, select all, and press erase (or delete permanently). Feel the instant gratification from seeing all those emails disappear.

» **You have a report due soon, but you find yourself watching videos.** Put away distractions and focus on just writing 250 words of your introduction. Once you're finished, read it over and let the feelings of accomplishment motivate you to write even more.

To get a shot of instant gratification whenever you need it, you can revisit past accomplishments. Don't let feelings of success pass you by. What have you achieved this week? What are your greatest achievements ever? These reminders of your success are an easily-accessed source of gratification. Personally, anytime I'm feeling discouraged about my blog, one of the things that turns my mood around is looking at my website and scrolling through the hundreds of posts. If I'm unmotivated to clean, just looking at the one part of the house that is tidy gives me a boost to get started. See how that works? Celebrate. Shout out a "woot" or a "yes." Do that silly little happy dance. It sure feels good, doesn't it?

SMALL LUXURIES

Small luxuries make life special; taking time to enjoy a cup of coffee every morning no matter how busy you are or a daily chat with your best friend or favorite colleague are luxuries. Without these little moments of bliss, the day can feel long and even boring, especially when you're faced with a busy schedule and a serious list of must-dos to accomplish. No one wants to head into a day filled with back-to-back meetings and deadlines without knowing there's an oasis ahead, where they can enjoy a break. Small luxuries sprinkled throughout your day help to keep you energized, focused, and motivated. Nobody wants to just work all day—we also have to take time to play. Small luxuries help maintain your balance, and you have to make sure they're an intentional part of your schedule.

Small luxuries work as incentives if you indulge only *after* getting something done. So, a bit of self-control and discipline is required for this to work. Let's use the honor system. Do you promise to only allow yourself a small luxury after you've put in the work? That you'll only treat yourself for all the effort you're putting in? You deserve it, after all. Plus, it's good for your productivity. You're pairing progress with pleasure: like homework and a movie, taxes and a tasty treat, or house cleaning and a phone call with a friend. But the progress has to come first.

Treat Yourself

What makes something luxurious is not its price tag, but the comfort it supplies you. What makes these luxuries small is not their size, but rather the ease with which you can access to them. You don't need to schedule days off, drive for three hours, or spend hundreds of dollars to enjoy these indulgences.

Not sure what your small luxuries should be? Think about what you enjoy doing and what little things make you feel as if you're on cloud nine (even for just a few minutes). Here are some ideas to help you decide.

> » SNACKS AND SWEETS: Why not treat yourself to something sweet, savory, or salty? This boost from a snack you love is sure to raise your mood, which you'll likely need throughout the day. Take a quick trip to the cafeteria, café, corner store, or vending machine.

» SOCIAL SETTINGS: Feeling lonely and isolated? We are social creatures, and having time to connect with someone we care about can make a big difference. Schedule some time to call a friend, catch up with a family member, or grab coffee with a coworker.

» SELF-CARE: When you're busy working hard and taking care of others, it's easy to forget about yourself. Take time off for whatever self-care means to you. That could be a facial mask, a smoothie, a massage, a nice hot bath, or whatever it is you need.

» SOLO ADVENTURE: Some alone time can be comforting if you spend the majority of your time with others. Go for a walk, visit a local park or a nearby art gallery, window shop in the mall—just go do something solo.

Develop your list of go-to little luxuries and use them to break up your day the next time you have a big task. Deploy your calendar and your time-blocking skills to be sure that you always have a small luxury to look forward to after putting in your work time. For example, if you need to do some bookkeeping, you might plan to organize documents for two hours (including breaks, of course), then go for a walk and get a coffee before returning to work for two more hours. The only condition for using this strategy is to promise yourself you'll put in the time, then enjoy your small luxury. Work, play, repeat—that's it.

BIG INDULGENCES

Let's up the ante. How do you celebrate your extra special victories, like achieving a major goal or crossing a massive to-do off your list? There's a time for instant gratification and small luxuries, but—thank goodness—there's also a time for even bigger rewards. You know what I'm talking about: those landmark moments that deserve to be celebrated properly. Handing in your last paper of the semester, paying off a big loan, launching an online business, or finally unpacking the last box in your new house . . . these are times when eating an ice cream or doing your now-iconic happy dance just don't feel like enough. You've worked harder than ever before to achieve these milestones, and you sure deserve to celebrate like it.

Creating a big reward or incentive for achieving a major task or goal should be part of your long-term commitment to conquering procrastination. Here's a pro-tip: Don't wait until you've reached the finish line to decide how you'll celebrate. Knowing that a big indulgence awaits you as a reward, you will shift your focus from your present to your future, helping motivate you to stay the course. That positive anticipation is the perfect counterbalance to the anxiety we can feel about a mountain of work that needs doing. Instead of focusing on the work, you can focus on your reward.

Big Win, Big Reward

How does this sound: Small wins get small luxuries, but big wins deserve big indulgences. What we're talking about is something special, something out of the ordinary. Something so indulgent that it allows you to separate yourself from everyday life for a while, to escape from the stress of always having to get things done. You need this every now and then—definitely not every day or week, but just when you need it most. What's yours?

Here are a few examples to get you dreaming:

» A BIG BUY: What's a pretty big purchase on your wish list? Give this buy some meaning by treating yourself to it after accomplishing something major. For example, you've spent the entire summer cleaning out the basement with 20 years worth of junk, so you treat yourself to a ping pong table you now have space for.

» BON VOYAGE: Is there a trip you've always wanted to take? What's on your bucket list? Near or far, take time off for exploration and adventure. For example, you've just completed a massive project at work that took countless hours of overtime, so you take the week off to go to Paris.

» **BEAUTY BREAKS:** How have you always wanted to pamper yourself? Take a relaxing and rejuvenating retreat at a spa. Let's say that you've been a stay-at-home parent for the last three years and you more than deserve a weekend away. Take it—the kids are big enough to be without you.

For every major milestone in my life, I've made time for big indulgences. After getting my undergraduate degree, I went to Europe for two months. After a big exam, I'd get my hair styled or buy an outfit. Do whatever elevates you and your goals to the next level. Big indulgences are also an opportunity to invest in yourself and your future. Get that laptop that you've wanted for school, buy that course to grow your business, or build that home gym. If it reignites your passion, then go for it.

Your first step is to identify your task or goal, the one that will bring the big indulgence at completion. What have you been working toward? How long will it take to achieve? Big indulgences work best with long-term projects, so you can build anticipation as well as save up for it or schedule time off. But please indulge responsibly and live within your means—there's absolutely no justification for going into debt here. Big indulgences aren't defined by their price tag; what matters is that you're giving yourself a reward you love.

BE ACCOUNTABLE

I'm sure you can remember an incident when you embarrassingly promised something to someone but didn't deliver, you forgot to finish a task, or maybe even forgot that it was due. This can be a horrible feeling. But when it's entirely your responsibility to get things done on time, it's on you when you drop the ball.

Accountability means taking responsibility and ownership for your actions (or lack of action). It means you take seriously getting things done, doing your part to meet deadlines, and accomplishing tasks without excuse. If you have an accountability partner, you have someone who will hold you to your obligations in a supportive way. Instead of trying to go it alone, an accountability buddy secures your success and your sanity. The right accountability partner will be there for you to hear you, gently nudge you forward, and help you keep going. They act like an incentive to keep you moving forward with your goals. You don't need to conquer your procrastination all by yourself. Let others in so they can encourage and motivate you, as well as keep you on track.

How to Find Your Accountability Partner

Once you start exploring, you'll probably find that there are people all around you who need accountability just as much as you do. Here are the top ways to find an accountability partner:

» **Ask a friend.** Do you have a friend who shares the same goals as you? What about someone who lives a similar life as you? For example, if you're a work-at-home parent, finding an accountability partner living the same lifestyle would offer you a sympathetic and supportive ear.

» **Talk to your family.** Have any close or extended family members expressed interest in connecting? Let your family know what you're working toward—a healthier diet, a fitness program, a crafting or organizing project—and ask if anyone would like to join you. Even if they themselves can't, they might know someone who can. Post your query in your family group chats, send out an email, and see who replies.

» **Join online interest groups.** What online communities could you join and socialize in? For example, if you're working on your fitness, there are endless online groups on social media platforms dedicated to getting fit. If your goal is career-related, there may be a professional association that can connect you with others.

Not sure how to frame your request? Write something like this: "Hey everyone, I'm Nadalie and I'm a Toronto-based blogger looking for an accountability partner. I'm committed to growing my traffic and email list and would love to do weekly check-ins with someone with similar goals. If you're interested, please reply or send me a direct message." Here's another example: "Hey, fam, I'm on a mission to lose 15 pounds this summer—anyone interested in joining me? We could do weekly calls, share meal ideas, and keep each other motivated. Let's get together and make this happen." That's all there is to it. Just keep it casual and discuss more details after you connect one-on-one.

Once you have someone in mind, you should be clear with each other about your goals, sharing what you're working toward and how often you want to check in. I strongly encourage weekly check-ins that take 15 minutes or less, ideally over the phone or in a video chat. In-person check-ins require more of a commitment and could be a challenge for both of you.

For your weekly check-ins, you'll want to ensure you share your goal for the coming week, what you're working on, and how things are going. It's easy to spend your 15 minutes just chit-chatting about life, especially with a friend or family member. Try giving your conversation an agenda, discussing the actual accountability part first. You may also want to consider establishing firm consequences for not meeting weekly goals. For example, you could establish that if you don't go to the gym three times a week, you'll owe the other person $100. Now that's taking full ownership for your inaction! Trust me, if you mess up once and it costs you, you'll never do it again.

REAL CONSEQUENCES

What'll happen if you don't beat procrastination? It's understandable that you don't want to think about it. But that discomfort, those negative emotions, can actually work to your advantage.

As we've discussed, all of us tend to avoid feeling negative emotions at all costs. Now that you've learned how to handle those emotions in a healthy way instead of letting them drive you into procrastination, it's time to give negative emotions a second look. Yes, the dark side has a bad reputation. But objectively, emotions are neither good nor bad—they simply balance each other out. Without sadness, happiness wouldn't be so sweet. Without fear, bravery wouldn't mean anything at all. And just as instant gratification can serve as an incentive, the negative emotions that once led you to procrastinate can motivate you to get things done.

As much as I'd love to tell you that the rewards will always get you moving and keep you going—they won't. Psychologists tell us that human behavior is equally motivated, if not more so, by a desire to avoid negative consequences. On any given day, almost everything you do, from brushing your teeth to eating your vegetables to wearing a seatbelt, even showing up to work on time and completing your assignments promptly, helps you avoid negative consequences. It's the same with your tasks and to-dos. You're conquering procrastination to achieve benefits and incentives but also to avoid the harmful consequences of not completing your tasks.

Real and permanent change happens when the fear of staying the same is greater than the fear of change. Fear is undoubtedly seen as a negative emotion, even though its primary function is to protect us and keep us safe (which is a good thing). What does this have to do with you and procrastination? It's simple: You need to know the very real consequences of not conquering procrastination. If you keep your approach to tasks and duties the same, it would mean continuing to put things off, missing deadlines, and living a stress-filled life on the edge. How would this limit your life? Where would this procrastination-filled lifestyle ultimately lead you?

The Costs of Inaction

It's time to examine the unpleasant consequences of keeping procrastination in your life. Don't worry, you're ready for this. Here are three ways to face the music:

> » **Ask "What if I don't do it?"** What will happen if you don't conquer procrastination? Think about your tasks, to-dos, and

goals as you reflect. For example, you've been putting off weeding the front lawn and the dandelions are taking over. If you don't take care of it soon, your lawn will be overgrown. You may need to spend money on a special lawn treatment or new yard tools.

» **Describe the worst-case scenario.** What's the worst possible thing that can happen? You probably already have the answer. For instance, you're a full-time student working part-time, and if you're unable to get your assignments done, you'll fail a course. If you miss a shift at work, you won't get paid.

» **Be honest with yourself.** What do you want to change about your life right now? Remind yourself of your goals and your reason for pursuing them. For example, you've been putting off starting a side hustle. You've known for months now that full-time income is not enough to make ends meet. Things would be better if you did something about it.

On a day-to-day basis, I find that negative consequences keep me moving forward more often than incentives ever could. Sure, I want to treat myself after accomplishing a task, and I do love that feeling of instant gratification. But I fight with all I've got to avoid bad consequences. Take writing this book, for instance. I'll relish the day when I'll hold the first copy in my hands, feeling that sense of pride, and I look forward to the big indulgences I'll allow myself after months of hard work. But it's thoughts of disappointing my editor, missing deadlines, and squandering this opportunity that keep me at my desk writing. No one wants to live a life of regret—I certainly don't.

Use your fear of consequences as a warning system to keep you safe from procrastination, like a flashing alarm reminding you that procrastination leads to nothing good. And trust me, sometimes when old habits try to resurrect themselves, you'll need this reminder. This typically happens when life gets crazy and when unexpected situations arise—around the holidays, perhaps, or when you're sick. It's easy to fall into old habits and routines when you are in a vulnerable position emotionally, physically, or mentally. When you find this happening, it's time to review the cost of giving into procrastination to remind yourself how much better your life is without it.

PLAY THE LONG GAME

Where do you see yourself five years from now? Too far? Okay, how about one year from today? Where will you be and how will your life be better? By now, I hope you've concluded that conquering procrastination is about more than just getting things done. You need priorities and goals, hopes and dreams that you're continually working toward. That's what keeps you going long-term. You have to be able to see the big picture, even if you're just taking little steps right now. You have to play the long game.

So, where will each of these baby steps lead you in the end? We all have a picture of what we dream our lives will be and who we will become. What's your long-term plan for your life? By now, you've made incredible progress toward kicking your procrastination habit for good. The strategies in this book have helped you work through the worst of it. And with your most urgent tasks managed, your motivation secured, your focus sharpened, and your incentives and consequences enumerated, you're able to look ahead. No longer bogged down by the stress and anxiety of a day-to-day life dominated by procrastination, you're free to plan the future, to envision what's next for you.

Meet Your Future You

It's time to look beyond just one or two moves ahead in your chess game against procrastination. As you focus on the future, here's some advice to keep in mind:

» **See your future self.** Use your powers of visualization to see yourself in the future. What do you look like? What's your day-to-day life like? Give yourself a story, see it, feel it, and believe it's possible. For example, if you're in college right now, see your future self as a graduate with the job of your dreams.

- » **Identify future benefits.** Recognize the benefits your life will have in the future. By doing something today, how are you changing your future? What benefits and privileges are you securing for yourself? Say, for instance, you're working toward a big promotion. Know what benefits you'll receive, such as higher pay and extra days off to spend with your family.

- » **Stay future-minded.** Progress beats perfection, and mistakes are just an opportunity to learn. Don't get lost in the day-to-day or lose sight of your future. You're going to win some, and you'll lose others, but no matter what, you will keep going. As long as you're still moving forward, you're on the right path. If you've been distracted and unfocused, procrastinating like crazy for the last week, forgive yourself and move forward.

Take time to journal or write about your long-term game plans, and track your progress along the way. As you build a record of past achievements, you'll be able to remind yourself just how far you've come. Discouragement will raise its ugly head sometimes—that's a fact of life. But if you have a solid conception of your long game, you will always motivate yourself to follow through. Can you think of a better incentive than reaching your bright and shiny future?

Looking ahead and playing the long game are powerful methods for conquering procrastination for good, and for one simple reason: Procrastination is a short-sighted behavior that offers momentary relief. Remember how we discussed that people who put things off lack a connection with their future selves? Keeping in touch with your long-term goals will help form real, tangible connections between your present self and your future you. Like every deposit into your savings account, you are rejecting procrastination, and you're taking care of your anticipated future needs, making things easier for tomorrow. When you play the long game, you see your commitment and continued hard work as a gift to yourself that you'll receive later.

CHAPTER 7

Looking Ahead

How do you feel now, knowing that you have the tools you need to conquer procrastination? Pretty good, right? Have confidence in yourself. You now possess the know-how to accomplish what you need to when you have to. Celebrate this moment and remember how amazing it feels.

And then roll up your sleeves, because you're just getting started. You're ready to move beyond the pages of this book and get things done in the real world.

As you work to build the strategies you've learned into lifelong habits, know that this, too, takes time. Be patient and understanding with yourself. You'll have days free of distraction where you're focused and on task, but you'll also have days when you'll fight to get motivated and be productive. That's life, my friend. The thing that really matters, in the end, is that you keep fighting and keep working even if you fall off track. To ensure you maintain productivity despite any challenge that comes your way, let's reinforce everything you've learned and plan your way forward.

Keep Your List Up to Date

Getting started and figuring out what you need to do and what you want to achieve are massive accomplishments. Never underestimate the power of making a list, setting priorities, setting goals, and planning ahead. You need to start with a road map to find your way forward, decide what steps you need to take, and determine the order to take them.

Procrastination thrives on disorganization and confusion, two things you've more than managed. If you ever feel overwhelmed, remember: You know exactly how to handle this. You can take control of the situation with a list and a plan. Grab a pen and paper, write it all down, find a place to start, and get your most critical tasks complete. Let's review this more closely.

MAINTAIN YOUR LIST

What are you working on next? What new tasks have come up for you? Anytime you feel overwhelmed, go back to your master list and sort your tasks by importance and urgency. Like a prized rose bush, it's important to maintain your master list of to-dos (see the Yes, Make a List strategy on page 24) by pruning off tasks you've completed and feeding it with new tasks as they arise. Your master list is your starting point; use it to plan your weeks, assign daily must-dos, schedule your time, and stay organized. Pull out the category 1 tasks to create daily must-do lists, and start each day with one must-do task that you'll accomplish no matter what.

KEEP YOUR PRIORITIES IN MIND

What means the most to you now? Have you been neglecting anything important? You need to keep your priorities in mind every day. When life gets busy, stressful, and overwhelming like it tends to, it's easy to lose sight of your priorities. Stay calm, remind yourself what's important, and then make the best choices. Revisit them as needed, and keep them front-of-mind—or written on the page—as you rank your master list.

DON'T BE AFRAID TO MAKE CHANGES

Goal setting and planning ahead serves you, not the other way around. Time often brings a fresh perspective; your goals and priorities can shift, and that's okay. That means things can take longer than anticipated, tasks can arise you never saw coming, and your goals can change. Sit with your list of goals from time to time when you need to reconnect with them.

Continue to Carve Out Time

The best time-management technique you could ever use is this: Complete one task at a time, at the time of day or night when you're at your best. When you feel overwhelmed and hyper-busy, never forget that you don't need more time to get everything done—you just need to use the time you already have more wisely. Use your calendar (page 42), take 10-minute baby steps (page 44), and keep on time blocking (page 46). Ten minutes of focused productivity beats a whole day filled with distractions. You're a time-management pro now, so carve out the time required to crush your to-dos and achieve your goals.

MANAGE YOUR TIME WISELY

Have you been updating your calendar? Are you scheduling your days properly? Don't just schedule tasks and due dates in your calendar once—keep updating it regularly. Make a habit of recording every significant obligation and deadline the moment you become aware of it. Consider your schedule as a balancing act between productive hours and regular breaks: taking a break is never a waste of time; rather, it's an investment in your productivity. Use the Pomodoro Technique (page 53) or time blocking to help with productivity.

TAKE YOUR TIME WITH SMALL STEPS

How much can you accomplish in 10 minutes? Remember, with just 10 minutes here or there, you can take small but impactful steps toward completing your work. And anytime you're faced with a particularly difficult or tedious task, instead of putting it off, break it down into smaller steps and get started on the first one.

THE TIME OF DAY MATTERS

Everyone has times in a given day when they're the most awake and alert. Remember to save these high-energy hours for your most important or difficult tasks. Tackle the hardest tasks first, as early in your schedule as possible (see Find the Right Time of Day on page 48). Remind yourself that by eating the frog (or doing the hard thing first), you not only free yourself from a day spent stressing out, but you've also ensured that the task is done no matter what else happens.

Maintain Your Motivation

Motivation is often credited for being what gets you started and keeps you going. You now know that through your actions and your mindset, you're able to create motivation whenever you need it. It's not a magical or mystical force that comes and goes as it pleases. And, its absence is no longer a good enough excuse for you to put things off.

To get things done and continue on this positive path, you will need to tap into your motivation every day. All you need to do is use your "why" (page 60), visualize success (page 62), reframe your inner monologue (page 67), or make a game of it (page 69). Remember: you are in complete control of your motivation.

LET "WHY" CONTROL THE CONVERSATION

Your "why" needs to be stronger than any other conviction in your mind. What's your "why"? What drives and motivates you? Turn to this motivation source when you feel doubts, limiting beliefs, and other procrastination-fueling thoughts trying to take control of your inner monologue. When you find yourself losing touch with your motivation, revisit the hard questions at the beginning of chapter 4.

VISUALIZING IS BELIEVING

What does success look and feel like for you? What's your vision of the future? When you're having a tough day or feeling discouraged, use visualization to reignite your motivation. Continue visualizing daily for five minutes or more, incorporating the practice into your routine. Don't forget that your vision board (page 64) is a powerful motivational tool. Ensure that it's displayed where you can see it daily. The more you see it, the more you'll believe it.

MAKE YOUR OWN MOTIVATION

No matter how unmotivated you're feeling, you can always make a game of it. Games can get you out of your head and over the first hurdle to action. Motivation is a state of mind that can be reached by adding an element of excitement or challenge for yourself. Call on your take-action ritual (page 71) to jump-start your engines whenever you need it.

Strive to Stay Focused

Motivation might get you started, but it's focus that helps you stay the course, and continued focus is the key to following through on all of your tasks. When your mind is completely engaged, you can accomplish more and do it faster.

Remember that the perfect conditions for productivity occur internally and externally: Talk yourself into it (page 78), use a redirecting mantra (page 80), and stick to singletasking (page 47). Let people know your intentions (page 76), create the right distraction-free environment (page 86), and just say no (page 88). Use these strategies to keep your focus locked on target, and procrastination will not find a way into your life.

TALK YOURSELF ON TRACK

You have learned to use your power to declutter your mind and keep yourself focused. If you're struggling to get started, talk yourself into it: Remind yourself why this task is important and why it's urgent. Use the 10 talking points on page 79, and review your goals, your vision, and your past successes. Once you've begun working, stay on track by using a redirecting mantra that quiets the distracting noise in your mind. Continue to use focusing quotes, lyrics, or phrases like *Focus* and *I can do this*.

CREATE A DISTRACTION-FREE ENVIRONMENT

Whether you're working from home, at school, or in the office, try to find a space that isolates you from others, and set physical reminders like a closed door or a "busy working" sign. Silence those distracting technologies like emails, alerts, and messenger apps. Multitasking is bad for productivity, especially with technology in the mix. So, stay focused for longer periods by singletasking and limiting task-switching.

LET PEOPLE KNOW AND JUST SAY NO

Protect your focus with honest communication to others in your life, and be sure that everyone around you knows when you're available and when you need to work uninterrupted. When someone asks for your time, evaluate their request with the criteria in the Just Start Saying No section (page 88). Be comfortable saying no to anything not urgent, important, or relevant to you. And promise me that you'll never feel guilty for setting these healthy boundaries.

Look for Incentives

You should be so proud of yourself, not just for going up against your procrastination and winning, but also for your commitment to continuing to do so. With more tasks to accomplish and goals to achieve in the years ahead, you have just as many incentives waiting to be enjoyed. Never forget that you're working hard, you're giving this all you've got, and your efforts and energy should be celebrated.

Make this commitment today: You will not only continue to keep yourself accountable but also stay excited. Don't let the joy of getting things done fade away; stay invested and engaged in your success. It's those extra special luxuries, small indulgences, and moments of gratification that keep you going long-term. Be brave and honest in considering the negative consequences of giving in to procrastination. And continue to play the long game, seeing how every move you make can be the right choice not just today, but for your future.

HAVE CELEBRATIONS OF ALL SIZES

How will you experience daily instant gratification? What small luxuries and big indulgences will you treat yourself to? It's up to you to keep your passion and dedication alive. Break up your days with moments of instant gratification; find new ways to release that feeling of joy and pride. Never let a week go by without at least one small luxury, if not a few. And lastly, save up for big indulgences; they're so worth the wait. Allow yourself to stay in the game long-term by continuing to celebrate your progress.

KEEP YOURSELF ACCOUNTABLE

Avoid the consequences of inaction by finding an accountability partner to share ongoing support and encouragement. Stay connected with weekly check-ins, sharing progress, changes, and goals for the future with each other. Your accountability partner will be invaluable as you conquer procrastination in the long-term, as you will be for them. There will be times when you'll need to hear someone other than yourself say *You've got this* or *You've come so far; keep going.* I won't be there with you, but they can be.

Final Thought:
Go Easy on Yourself

You're not the same procrastinator you were when you started this book. Today you are a productive action-taker who has overcome the beliefs and behaviors that were holding you back.

There's one bit of advice that I've saved for the end. I hope that as much as you remember anything from this book, it's this: *Always forgive yourself for procrastinating.* Forgiveness is your escape route from the cycle of procrastination and guilt. An encouraging 2010 study found that students who forgave themselves for procrastinating in the past were less likely to do it again. Anytime you find yourself drifting in a storm of delay, anchor yourself in forgiveness. Let forgiveness free you of any regrets for putting things off and push you forward into productive positivity. When you forgive yourself, procrastination doesn't stand a chance!

Conquering procrastination is a daily choice. It isn't a one-time fix. And it's a choice that I hope you wake up every day ready to make. Getting things done on time, without excuses, is a skill that takes practice to master. So, get to it, and if you ever lose your focus, don't lose more time consumed by your mistakes; you know those times when you might be distracted or have unproductive days. Learn to let it go and always keep moving forward.

RESOURCES

Books

If you're looking for more ways to conquer procrastination, the following books are worth reading.

Eat That Frog! 21 Great Ways to Stop Procrastinating and Get More Done in Less Time by Brian Tracy.

Self-Discipline in 6 Weeks: How to Build Goals with Soul and Make Your Habits Work for You by Jennifer Webb.

Solving the Procrastination Puzzle: A Concise Guide to Strategies for Change by Timothy A. Pychyl.

Still Procrastinating? The No-Regrets Guide to Getting It Done by Joseph R. Ferrari.

The 5 Second Rule: Transform Your Life, Work, and Confidence with Everyday Courage by Mel Robbins.

The Procrastination Equation: How to Stop Putting Things Off and Start Getting Stuff Done by Piers Steel.

Websites & Apps

For a deeper dive into improving your productivity and learning about mental wellness:

It's All You Boo: ItsAllYouBoo.com

Continue your journey over at my blog, where you'll find helpful strategies for goal-setting, finding motivation, increasing productivity, improving mental health, creating good habits, inspirational quotes, and more. Join my free VIP resource library, which has over 25 quizzes, printables, workbooks, and challenges on just about everything you need.

Psychology Today: PsychologyToday.com

Learn more about the psychological side of procrastination and a wide range of other topics. All their articles are written by reputable professionals who know what they're talking about. You can also connect with local therapists and counsellors.

Try these websites to manage your time more wisely by delegating less important tasks, from household chores to business duties:

Fiverr: Fiverr.com

Handy: Handy.com

TaskRabbit: TaskRabbit.com

Thumbtack: Thumbtack.com

Share your schedule and plan your calendar with these applications:

Apple or Google Calendar: Available on your desktop or mobile device.

Asana: Asana.com

Cozi Family Organizer: Cozi.com

Trello: Trello.com

The following tools can help you find images for your digital vision board. Be sure to read the fine print and understand each site's photo-release policy before using images.

Online Graphic Design and Collage Tools:

» Canva: Canva.com

» MilaNote: MilaNote.com

» Pinterest: Pinterest.com

Free Stock Photo Sites:

» Pexels: Pexels.com

» Pixabay: Pixabay.com

» Unsplash: Unsplash.com

These popular extensions for the Chrome browser can help you avoid distractions like advertisements and news feeds:

AdBlock Plus: AdBlockPlus.org

Google Chrome Extensions:

» AdBlock: GetAdBlock.com/chrome

» Kill News Feed Chrome: bit.ly/killnewsfeed

» Momentum: MomentumDash.com

» StayFocusd: bit.ly/stayfocusd

Use these break timer and Pomodoro apps to set your schedule, rest your eyes, and take regular breaks throughout the day:

Focus Booster: FocusBoosterApp.com

Focus To-Do: FocusToDo.cn

Focus Keeper: bit.ly/focuskeeper

Use the following resources to take a closer look at the Eisenhower Matrix for ranking tasks, including a video, free printables, and more.

Eisenhower Matrix: Eisenhower.me/eisenhower-matrix

Focus Matrix Application for Apple Devices: bit.ly/focusmatrix

Ike - To-Do List, Task List Application for Android: bit.ly/iketodo

Conduct a time audit using these applications:

Applications (also available via your device's app store):

» Harvest: GetHarvest.com

» HoursTracker: HoursTrackerApp.com

» Hours Time Tracking: HoursTimeTracking.com

» Punch Time Clock: TrentMorris.com/punch

Physical Time Tracker:

» Timeular: Timeular.com

REFERENCES

American Psychological Association. "Multitasking: Switching costs." March 20, 2006. Apa.org/research/action/multitask.

Anderson, Tyler. "Dr. Piers Steel on the Procrastination Equation." *The National Post*. January 17, 2011. NationalPost.com/afterword /dr-piers-steel-on-the-procrastination-equation.

Association for Psychological Science. "Inner Speech Speaks Volumes About the Brain." July 16, 2013. PsychologicalScience.org/news /releases/internal-speech-is-driven-by-predictive-brain-signal.html.

Batcho, Krystine I. "What Are You Waiting For?" *Psychology Today*. December 21, 2019. PsychologyToday.com/us/blog/longing -nostalgia/201912/what-are-you-waiting.

Berkman, Elliot T. "Why Wait? The Psychological Origins of Procrasti-nation." *Psychology Today*. October 8, 2015. PsychologyToday.com /us/blog/the-motivated-brain/201510/why-wait-the-psychological -origins-procrastination.

Berkovich-Ohana, Aviva, Meytal Wilf, Roni Kahana, Amos Arieli, and Rafael Malach. "Repetitive speech elicits widespread deactivation in the human cortex: the "Mantra" effect?" *Brain and Behavior* 5, no. 7 (July 2015): doi:10.1002/brb3.346.

Bhali, Gill. "New To Visualization? Here Are 5 Steps To Get You Started." *Forbes*. June 22, 2017. Forbes.com/sites/bhaligill/2017/06 /22/new-to-visualization-here-are-5-steps-to-get-you-started /#655eac4d6e3f.

Blouin-Hudon, Eve-Marie C. and Timothy A. Pychyl. "Experiencing the temporally extended self: Initial support for the role of affective states, vivid mental imagery, and future self-continuity in the prediction of academic procrastination." *Personality and Individual Differences* 86 (November 2015): 50–66. doi:10.1016/j.paid.2015.06.003.

Boyes, Alice. "Seven Self-Sabotaging Things Perfectionists Do." *Psychology Today.* July 19, 2018. PsychologyToday.com/us/blog /in-practice/201807/seven-self-sabotaging-things-perfectionists-do.

Canfield, Jack. "Visualization Techniques to Affirm Your Desired Outcomes: A Step-by-Step Guide." Accessed March 4, 2020. JackCanfield.com/blog/visualize-and-affirm-your-desired-outcomes -a-step-by-step-guide.

Cherry, Kendra. "The Psychology of Procrastination." Last modified June 30, 2019. VeryWellMind.com/the-psychology-of-procrastination -2795944.

Cherry, Kendra. "Tips for Overcoming Procrastination." Last modified August 18, 2019. VeryWellMind.com/tips-for-overcoming -procrastination-2795714.

Cirillo, Francesco. "The Pomodoro Technique." Accessed March 10, 2020. FrancescoCirillo.com/pages/pomodoro-technique.

Collins Dictionary. "Akrasia." Accessed February 8, 2020. CollinsDictionary.com/dictionary/english/akrasia.

Dalla-Camina, Megan. "The Reality of Imposter Syndrome." *Psychology Today.* September 3, 2018. PsychologyToday.com/us/blog/real-women /201809/the-reality-imposter-syndrome.

Dictionary.com. "Akrasia." Accessed February 8, 2020. Dictionary .com/browse/akrasia.

Dudeja, Jai. "Scientific Analysis of Mantra-Based Meditation and Its Beneficial Effects: An Overview." *International Journal of Advanced Scientific Technologies in Engineering and Management Sciences* 3, no. 6 (June 2017): 21–6. doi:10.22413/ijastems/2017/v3/i6/49101.

Duhigg, Charles. "How Habits Work." Accessed February 11, 2020. CharlesDuhigg.com/how-habits-work.

Ferrari, Joseph R., Judith L Johnson, and William G. McCown. *Procrastination and Task Avoidance–Theory, Research, and Treatment*. New York: Plenum Press, 1995.

Ferrari, Joseph R. "Psychology of Procrastination: Why People Put Off Important Tasks Until the Last Minute." American Psychological Association. April 5, 2010. Apa.org/news/press/releases/2010/04/procrastination.

Flett, Gordon L., Murray Stainton, Paul L. Hewitt, Simon B. Sherry, and Clarry Lay. "Procrastination Automatic Thoughts as a Personality Construct: An Analysis of the Procrastinatory Cognitions Inventory." *Journal of Rational-Emotive and Cognitive-Behavior Therapy* 30, no. 4 (March 20, 2012): 223–236. doi:10.1007/s10942-012-0150-z.

Gambino, Megan. "Why Procrastination Is Good for You." *Smithsonian Magazine*. July 12, 2012. SmithsonianMag.com/science-nature/why-procrastination-is-good-for-you-2102008.

Garcy, Pamela D. "9 Reasons You Procrastinate (and 9 Ways to Stop)." *Psychology Today.* June 16, 2015. PsychologyToday.com/us/blog/fearless-you/201506/9-reasons-you-procrastinate-and-9-ways-stop.

Gillihan, Seth J. "Why It's Easy to Procrastinate—and 7 Ways to Break the Habit." *Psychology Today.* December 12, 2016. Psychology Today.com/us/blog/think-act-be/201612/why-its-easy-procrastinate-and-7-ways-break-the-habit.

Griffey, Harriet. "The Lost Art of Concentration: Being Distracted in a Digital World." The Guardian. October 14, 2018. TheGuardian.com/lifeandstyle/2018/oct/14/the-lost-art-of-concentration-being-distracted-in-a-digital-world.

Grund, Axel, and Stefan Fries. "Understanding Procrastination: A Motivational Approach." *Personality and Individual Differences* 121 (January 2018): 120–30. doi:10.1016/j.paid.2017.09.035.

Hershfield, Hal E. "Future Self-Continuity: How Conceptions of the Future Self Transform Intertemporal Choice." *Decision Making Over the Life Span* 1235, no. 1 (September 6, 2013) 30–43. doi:10.1111%2Fj.1749-6632.2011.06201.x.

Ho, Leon. "What Is Procrastination and How to Stop It (The Complete Guide)." Lifehack. Last modified February 11, 2020. Lifehack.org/669901/how-to-stop-procrastinating.

Ho, Leon. "Why Do I Procrastinate? 5 Root Causes & How To Tackle Them." Lifehack. Last modified January 2, 2020. Lifehack.org/articles/lifehack/6-reasons-on-why-are-you-procrastinating.html.

Jaffe, Eric. "Why Wait? The Science Behind Procrastination." Association for Psychological Science. March 29, 2013. PsychologicalScience.org/observer/why-wait-the-science-behind-procrastination.

Kruse, Kevin. "The Truth Behind Why We Procrastinate." *Forbes*. February 23, 2016. Forbes.com/sites/kevinkruse/2016/02/23/the-truth-behind-why-we-procrastinate/#2037dbdc16cc.

Lin, Lin. "Breadth-Biased Versus Focused Cognitive Control in Media Multitasking Behaviors." *Proceedings of the National Academy of Science of the United States of America* 106, no. 37 (September 15, 2009): 15521–22. doi:10.1073/pnas.0908642106.

Matthews, Gail. "Goals Research Summary." Dominican University. Accessed March 21, 2020. Dominican.edu/sites/default/files/2020-02/gailmatthews-harvard-goals-researchsummary.pdf.

Mayo Clinic. "Adult attention-deficit/hyperactivity disorder (ADHD)." June 22, 2019. MayoClinic.org/diseases-conditions/adult-adhd/symptoms-causes/syc-20350878.

Mayo Clinic. "Anxiety disorders." May 4, 2018. MayoClinic.org/diseases-conditions/anxiety/symptoms-causes/syc-20350961.

Mayo Clinic. "Depression (major depressive disorder)." February 3, 2018. MayoClinic.org/diseases-conditions/depression/symptoms-causes/syc-20356007.

Mayo Clinic. "Obsessive-compulsive disorder (OCD)." March 11, 2020. MayoClinic.org/diseases-conditions/obsessive-compulsive -disorder/symptoms-causes/syc-20354432.

Mayo Clinic. "Stress symptoms: Effects on your body and behavior." April 4, 2019. MayoClinic.org/healthy-lifestyle/stress-management /in-depth/stress-symptoms/art-20050987.

McBride, Karyl. "Are You Plagued With Self-Doubt?" *Psychology Today.* April 18, 2011. PsychologyToday.com/us/blog/the-legacy -distorted-love/201104/are-you-plagued-self-doubt.

Merriam-Webster. "Procrastinate." Accessed February 8, 2020. Merriam-Webster.com/dictionary/procrastinate.

Middlebrooks, Catherine and Castel, Alan. "Focused Distractions? How We Adapt to Multi-Tasking." *Psychology Today.* July 31, 2017. PsychologyToday.com/us/blog/metacognition-and-the-mind/201707 /focused-distractions-how-we-adapt-multi-tasking.

Millett, Maria. "Challenge your negative thoughts." Michigan State University Extension. March 31, 2017. Canr.msu.edu/news/challenge _your_negative_thoughts.

Moran, Susan. "The Science Behind Finding Your Mantra and How to Practice It Daily." *Yoga Journal.* Last modified November 12, 2018. YogaJournal.com/yoga-101/mantras-101-the-science-behind-finding -your-mantra-and-how-to-practice-it.

Nadeau, Kathleen. "Over-committed, Over-extended and Over- whelmed." *Psychology Today.* November 27, 2013. PsychologyToday .com/us/blog/the-distraction-wars/201311/over-committed-over -extended-and-overwhelmed.

Nemko, Marty. "Time Management and Procrastination: What Works." *Psychology Today.* December 8, 2019. PsychologyToday.com/us /blog/how-do-life/201912/time-management-and-procrastination -what-works.

Patel, Neil. "When, How, and How Often to Take a Break." *Inc.* December 11, 2014. Inc.com/neil-patel/when-how-and-how-often-to-take-a-break.html.

Price-Mitchell, Marilyn. "Goal-Setting Is Linked to Higher Achievement." *Psychology Today*. March 14, 2018. PsychologyToday.com/us/blog/the-moment-youth/201803/goal-setting-is-linked-higher-achievement.

Psychology Today. "Default Mode Network." Accessed March 7, 2020. PsychologyToday.com/us/basics/default-mode-network.

Psychology Today. "Self-Talk." Accessed March 5, 2020. PsychologyToday.com/us/basics/self-talk.

Pychyl, Timothy A. "Giving in to Feel Good: Why Self-regulation Fails." *Psychology Today*. April 25, 2008. PsychologyToday.com/us/blog/dont-delay/200804/giving-in-feel-good-why-self-regulation-fails.

Pychyl, Timothy A. "How Negative Thoughts Relate to Procrastination." *Psychology Today*. March 8, 2018. PsychologyToday.com/us/blog/dont-delay/201803/how-negative-thoughts-relate-procrastination.

Pychyl, Timothy A. "Procrastination: Motivation Deficit vs. Regulation Failure." *Psychology Today*. June 12, 2019. PsychologyToday.com/us/blog/dont-delay/201906/procrastination-motivation-deficit-vs-regulation-failure.

Reynolds, Susan. "Happy Brain, Happy Life." *Psychology Today*. August 2, 2011. PsychologyToday.com/us/blog/prime-your-gray-cells/201108/happy-brain-happy-life.

Rock, David. "Easily Distracted?" *Psychology Today*. October 4, 2009. PsychologyToday.com/us/blog/your-brain-work/200910/easily-distracted.

Selig, Meg. "How Do Work Breaks Help Your Brain? 5 Surprising Answers." *Psychology Today*. April 18, 2017. PsychologyToday.com/us/blog/changepower/201704/how-do-work-breaks-help-your-brain-5-surprising-answers.

Sirois, Fuschia M., and Timothy A. Pychyl. "Procrastination and the Priority of Short-Term Mood Regulation: Consequences for Future Self." *Social and Personality Psychology Compass* 7, no. 2 (February 2013): 115–27. doi:10.1111/spc3.12011.

Sirois, Fuschia M. "Procrastination and Stress: Exploring the Role of Self-compassion." *Self and Identity* 13, no. 2 (February 2013): 128–45. doi:10.1080/15298868.2013.763404.

Steel, Piers. "The Nature of Procrastination: A Meta-Analytic and Theoretical Review of Quintessential Self-Regulatory Failure." *Psychological Bulletin* 133, no. 1 (February 2007): 65–94. doi:10.1037/0033-2909.133.1.65.

Steel, Piers. "The True Meaning of Procrastination." *Psychology Today.* December 2, 2010. PsychologyToday.com/us/blog/the -procrastination-equation/201012/the-true-meaning-procrastination.

Stein, Traci. "Kicking the Procrastination 'Habit'." *Psychology Today.* March 13, 2013. PsychologyToday.com/us/blog/the-integrationist /201303/kicking-the-procrastination-habit.

Svartdal, Frode, Sjur Granmo and Fredrik S. Færevaag. "On the Behavioral Side of Procrastination: Exploring Behavioral Delay in Real-Life Settings." *Frontiers in Psychology* 16, no. 9 (May 16, 2018): 746. doi:10.3389/fpsyg.2018.00746.

Swanson, Ana. "The real reasons you procrastinate—and how to stop." *Washington Post.* April 27, 2016. WashingtonPost.com/news /wonk/wp/2016/04/27/why-you-cant-help-read-this-article-about -procrastination-instead-of-doing-your-job.

Tice, Dianne M., and Roy F. Baumeister. "Longitudinal Study of Procrastination, Performance, Stress, and Health: The Costs and Benefits of Dawdling. American Psychological Science. November 6, 1997. Amherst.edu/media/view/230062/original/procrastinating.pdf.

Tracy, Brian. "Eat That Frog: Brian Tracy Explains The Truth About Frogs." *Brian Tracy International (blog).* Accessed February 24, 2020. BrianTracy.com/blog/time-management/the-truth-about-frogs.

Trapani, Gina. "Work Smart: Do Your Worst Task First (Or, Eat a Live Frog Every Morning)." *Fast Company*. March 22, 2010. Fast Company.com/1592454/work-smart-do-your-worst-task-first-or -eat-live-frog-every-morning.

Wei, Marlynn. "How Mantras Calm Your Mind." *Psychology Today*. August 14, 2015. PsychologyToday.com/us/blog/urban-survival /201508/how-mantras-calm-your-mind.

White, Martha C. "The Exact Perfect Amount of Time to Take a Break, According to Data." *Time*. October 20, 2014. Time.com /3518053/perfect-break.

Whitbourne, Susan Krauss. "A New Way to Understand Procrastina- tion." *Psychology Today*. January 9, 2018. PsychologyToday.com /us/blog/fulfillment-any-age/201801/new-way-understand -procrastination.

Whitbourne, Susan Krauss. "12 Ways to Beat Procrastination." *Psychology Today*. November 12, 2016. PsychologyToday.com/us /blog/fulfillment-any-age/201611/12-ways-beat-procrastination.

Widrich, Leo. "Why We Have Our Best Ideas in the Shower: The Science of Creativity." *Buffer (blog)*. Last modified September 7, 2018. Open.Buffer.com/shower-thoughts-science-of-creativity.

Wiegartz, Pamela. "Why Do You Procrastinate?" *Psychology Today*. March 25, 2011. PsychologyToday.com/us/blog/in-the-age-anxiety /201103/why-do-you-procrastinate.

Williams, Caroline. "Five Ways Science Can Improve Your Focus." BBC Worklife. September 24, 2017. BBC.com/worklife/article /20170925-the-surprising-tricks-to-help-you-focus-at-work.

Winch, Guy. "10 Real Risks of Multitasking, to Mind and Body." *Psychology Today*. June 22, 2016. PsychologyToday.com/us/blog /the-squeaky-wheel/201606/10-real-risks-multitasking-mind-and-body.

Winch, Guy. "10 Signs That You Might Have Fear of Failure." *Psychology Today.* June 18, 2013. PsychologyToday.com/us/blog /the-squeaky-wheel/201306/10-signs-you-might-have-fear-failure.

Wohl, Michael J.A., Timothy A. Pychyl, Shannon H. Bennett. "I Forgive Myself, Now I Can Study: How Self-Forgiveness for Procrastinating Can Reduce Future Procrastination." *Personality and Individual Differences* 48, no. 7 (May 2010): 803–8. doi:10.1016 /j.paid.2010.01.029.

INDEX

ACKNOWLEDGMENTS

I've always believed that one moment can change your life. I'm so grateful to my publisher, Callisto Media, for seeing this book in me before I even imagined it. To Samantha Holland, my editor and Jedi Master, you're simply the best. Thank you for transforming this blogger into an author. A special shout-out to Rick Chillot: You're the King of Clarity—thank you. I am so grateful for the entire Callisto team, from the designers to the copyeditors: thank you for creating such a beautiful book.

To the psychologists and experts in the field of procrastination and productivity: This book stands on your shoulders and is a love letter to your decades of research. Your commitment to helping us understand procrastination is inspiring. Without your expertise and guidance, I would never have known where to start. On behalf of all the procrastinators around the world, thank you for helping us get things done.

G'ma, I wish you were here so I could thank you in person. I was able to type every word of this book because of your last gift to me. Thank you for getting me here. Many more thanks to my family and friends, who contributed their tips and continued support along the way. Lastly, to my accountability buddy Carly, thanks for all the em dashes and for keeping me sane. I dedicate this book to all of you!

ABOUT THE AUTHOR

NADALIE BARDO is a content creator committed to helping you live your best life with confidence and action. After working full-time in a career job, Nadalie quit the 9-to-5 life to pursue her passion as a self-employed entrepreneur. As the founder of *It's All You Boo*, a personal development blog, she curates the very best content to keep you motivated and inspired to slay your goals in life and business. Nadalie is also the creator of the *Slay Your Goals Planner*, a planner dedicated to helping you actually achieve your goals.

In a previous life, Nadalie pursued a career in public relations. She holds a master's degree in development studies from York University in Toronto, Canada, and a post-graduate's diploma in corporate communications and public relations. Merging her past with her passions, Nadalie also works with bloggers, brands, and businesses to navigate the online world of social media marketing and content creation. No matter the circumstances—in the home, office, college, or life—Nadalie is dedicated to helping everyone she can live the life they've always imagined.